No Quarter November

No Quarter November

THE 2019 ANTHOLOGY

DOUGLAS WILSON

canonpress
Moscow, Idaho

Published by Canon Press
P.O. Box 8729, Moscow, ID 83843
800.488.2034 | www.canonpress.com

Douglas Wilson, *No Quarter November: The 2019 Anthology*
Copyright © 2020 by Douglas Wilson.

Printed in the United States of America.
Cover design by James Engerbretson.

Library of Congress Cataloging-in-Publication Data Forthcoming

20 21 22 23 24 25 26 27   10 9 8 7 6 5 4 3 2 1

To C.R. Wiley,
who watching the making of the trailer unafraid,
and who accurately described from across the country,
on Facebook of all places,
our desire to move the Overton Window

Contents

NQN, Part Deux

Well, here it is, November once more. Many of you know the drill since I did this last year. But mark, you only know the drill if I do the same basic thing I did last year, which I *intend* to, but you didn't necessarily know that, did you? And on top of that, some of you are new.

Here's the deal. I do understand that I write provocatively from time to time. But there are different ways to be provocative. For example, there is the cudgeling style that might be employed by one of the Nephilim laying about him on every side with a Juvenalian quarterstaff. There is no real nuance in that kind of mayhem. Then there is the little Horatian pinprick wound made by one of those dentistry tools, that thing with the little tiny wire on the end of it. That does have nuance and subtlety. My difficulty is that my tone—whenever I shift gears away from my standard oleaginous docility—is Horatian, and yet a number of people tend to mistake it for the quarterstaff treatment.

So what I usually try to do is this. I (*usually*) know if something is going to go over big, and so I take care to pack, nice and tidy like, a number of disclaimers and qualifications early on in the piece, usually in the second paragraph. These anticipatory qualifications take care to inform the world that, "no, I don't believe that all women are stupid," for example. I have to make this kind of qualification because it is possible that I am about to maintain, in the course of my upcoming argument, that most men are taller than most women. This, naturally, opens me up to the charge of maintaining that all women are stupid. I try to anticipate such things, and disavow them beforehand.

Of course, with a certain class of critic this careful approach does not work at all. They blow right past my qualifications, *as though they didn't even exist.* And then what have I done? I will tell you what that does. It exasperates those readers who have followed me for years, and who by this point could almost write my qualifications for me. These poor souls dance in place, they yell at the ceiling, they shake their forefinger at the computer screen, and all for naught. There I go again, qualifying my position, as though someone were reading carefully.

Except for November. This November, just like last November, I might as well be hanged for a sheep as for a lamb. I will just say what I think. I will not try to anticipate any blowbacky outrage, and I will not hedge any of my bets. But this is not really my version of Rand Paul's celebration of Festivus, where he "airs his grievances." No, the grievances are always aired. That part is dialed in over eleven months. What is new is that for one month I will treat my most hostile critics to one full month of confirmation bias. I will write me the way they read me. Will it make any difference? Not a bit, except to my friends, who have been telling me how much they are looking forward to November.

CHAPTER ONE

Inerrancy as the Queen Mum of Evangelicalism

Secularists scoff at the Bible. Postmodernists sneer at the metanarrative for not being their own. And liberals cherry pick what *they* find to be of lasting spiritual value, according to the canons of the very latest contagions from the academy. And in the face of such manifest unbelief, conservative inerrantists draw themselves up to their full height in order to *pretend* to believe the Bible. And of course, the appearance given by such stated conviction also provides an appearance of courage, which was perhaps the point.

Inerrancy is the queen mum of evangelicals—honored, respected, and praised in the abstract, while entirely ignored when it comes to practical obedience. Ignored, that is, unless it is one of those special holidays where she is trundled out onto a balcony to wave at her loyal sons and daughters below. Correction: make that her disloyal sons and daughters. Folks are willing to show up periodically to be waved at by the Chicago Statement, but that is the full extent of their commitment. Inerrancy appears to have nothing to do with issues like authority and obedience. Inerrancy is only there to beam at us while we continue to do whatever we took it into our heads to do.

Cooking for Pigs

Let us suppose—and these dark days it is not that big a suppose—that you wanted to advance some godforsaken pig's breakfast in the name of Jesus, and there was an outcry from some of the predictable types—you know, the ones with a critical spirit and a censorious eye. And so it suddenly became your desire to get them to lay off. All you have to do is get out your tube of Critic-B-Gone, now available at Walgreens, and slather a bit of that "I am deeply committed to inerrancy" cream on your forearms. *Ta da*, as the kids say.

So long as you are committed to the inerrancy of the Bible you never have to do anything that it says.

This is why secularists and liberals, who are not committed to inerrancy, are often more to be trusted with what the Scriptures actually say because they are not ever stuck with defending the final results. They can say, for example, that the apostle Paul told certain busybody women to "go home" (Tit. 2:5) and wasn't *that* just a laugh riot? So the unbeliever can just flow with the spirit of the age. He can simply walk along in step with that spirit, letting his arms swing free. The professed evangelical, on the other hand, has beads of sweat appearing upon his brow as he breaks out the usually reliable Greek word study. Unfortunately, he has needed to rely on these things more and more as the madness of our age has been moving into its more frenzied and spastic stages. And speaking of stages, what stage is it when your exegesis is flat on its back, heels drumming on the floor?

But fortunately, the word there in Titus is *oikourgos*, which one could perhaps even render as "bossy pants." Indeed, Twila Fitzhearst Simmons, EdD, has made precisely this application, both in her monographs and in her personal life.

The Law is Holy, Righteous, and Good

Fortunately for those engaged in this strategy of sanctified shiftiness, they can rely on massive amounts of biblical ignorance in the evangelical ranks. You can get away with a *lot* when nobody is reading their Bible. You hardly ever have to answer any questions.

> As for your male and female slaves whom you may have: you may buy male and female slaves from among the nations that are around you. You may also buy from among the strangers who sojourn with you and their clans that are with you, who have been born in your land, and they may be your property. You may bequeath them to your sons after you to inherit as a possession forever. You may make slaves of them, but over your brothers the people of Israel you shall not rule, one over another ruthlessly. (Lev. 25:44–46, ESV)

Let us ask and answer some exegetical questions now, and try not to make any faces while we do this. Was it lawful and proper for an Israelite—let's call him Jonathan Edwards, or perhaps even @johnhsather, just for grins—to buy an Amalekite for a slave? Further, was it lawful and proper for an Israelite to buy an Amalekite slave whose family had lived in Israel for three generations already? Why yes, it was. And if such a transaction occurred, what relationship would have then existed between the master and his slave? Would it be appropriate to say that verse 45 says that the Israelite owned an Amalekite *as his personal property*?

"Let us continue," the Sunday School teacher says, even though the eyes of the class are now the size of teacup saucers. Was it lawful and proper for whichever Jonathan to bequeath these slaves to his heirs and assigns? And how long was this state of affairs to last? Can we find the word *forever* in the text? Well, yes, right there in verse 46. So we are talking about a form of permanent slavery, is that correct?

Oh, but we have various devices to deal with this. We have our hand-waving strategies down pat. We say, and all together now, but that's in the *Old* Testament. Okay, that is in the Old Testament. I knew that because I put the reference down. It is from Leviticus. But was it, for that time, under those circumstances, holy, righteous, and good (Rom. 7:12)? This is a law, straight from God. Was it a good law? Or a bad law? Do you approve of it? Or does the holiness of God conflict with all your Enlightenment assumptions that you mistook for holiness?

That Amalekite slave, and his children, and his grandchildren, have all been dead for a long time now. But they all died in slavery. So I would like ask my fellow inerrantists to step up to the microphone and tell everyone—particularly the atheists, about whom a bit more in a few minutes—whether they approve of this law in its original setting. If you don't, your commitment to inerrancy is what men of another age would have called a Joke. If you do approve of it, then let us pause for a few moments while all the evangelical thought leaders block you on Twitter.

Those guys crack me up.

And Jesus Was No Woke Buttercup

In the parable of the unforgiving servant (Matt. 18:21-35)—"but-that's-in-the-Old . . . *wait*"—we should begin by noting how often our translators pitch in to help us out of our sob-sister difficulties. The word *servants* brings to mind the halcyon world of *Downton Abbey* instead of slaves from the grim world of Simon Legree. But these are not servants in the sense of the hired help—they are slaves. Notice how the master was going to resolve the problem of indebtedness by selling his slave off, along with the wife and kids (Matt. 18:25). You don't sell off the hired help. Or, if you do, it is generally frowned upon.

In addition, at the conclusion of the story, the master, instead of selling him, turns him over to the *basanistes*. In the ancient world, torture of slaves was not uncommon, but it was not so common that every master felt he had to own his own gear. So what developed was a system of renting a professional—someone who owned the thumbscrews and all, and who could bring everything around to your place whenever it was needed. Kind of like Windshield Doctor. These professionals with the right equipment for every slave-owner's needs were called the *basanistes*. The ESV helpfully obscures this for tender inerrantists by calling them *jailers*.

And so we mutter, *sotto voce*, that of course Jesus did take illustrations from everyday life, from time to time, and which could include things like this, which does not necessarily imply endorse . . . but then He interrupts us, wrapping the parable up like this.

"So likewise shall my heavenly Father do also unto you, if ye from your hearts forgive not every one his brother their trespasses" (Matt. 18:35).

Atheist for a Year?

If I ever attained to the seared conscience that some folks think I already have, and if I wanted to pay off the mortgage of my house really quick, I could renounce the faith (but only for a year or two), declare myself an outspoken atheist, and challenge evangelical believers everywhere to debate, to come and defend their precious Book. "Tell me," I would say in my opening statement, "are you committed to inerrancy? Because I would like to use the remainder of my time by reading some Bible verses out loud."

Now the faith as it stands in its glorious historical reality is solid and massive, immoveable, and quite capable of making every orc in Mordor quail. The gates of Hades will not prevail against her. But the kind of jiggery pokery that goes on in modern apologetics presents quite a different picture. It is rare to find true biblical apologists anymore. Instead we have PR hacks, with one eye on the authoritative vagaries of public opinion and the other eye on the main chance. That is not the fortress of the true faith. No, *that* is a Disney castle, with gigantic Styrofoam blocks, and one that could probably be taken out by an aggressive atheist sophomore with some kindling and a Bic lighter.

So claiming to believe in inerrancy—that glorious abstraction, all rise!—whenever you are called on to explain your most recent tomfoolery is not the same thing as living under the authority of Scripture. The Bible is not simply "without error." The Bible is without error *and* is the final and complete and ultimate and absolute Word of authority that supersedes all the dumb stuff that our theological thought leaders manage to cook up with such regularity. But also remember that the only reason they can cook so much is that the pigs are always hungry.

So while Christians should of course work through the challenge of harmonizing Scripture with Scripture, and one scriptural principle with another, we have no obligation whatever to harmonize Scripture with the bruised feelings of the bed wetters, the harpies, or the bellygods.

But in the meantime, all the modern Christians lament together. Why do secular nonbelievers refuse to believe the Bible? I hate to break it to everybody, but *they* refuse because the Christians are also refusing to do so. Nobody wants to deal with the Bible *as it is*. Why should unbelievers believe what the believers won't believe? It seems to me that when it comes to believing, the believers should go first.

Non-Christians don't believe the Bible. So? *The Christians don't believe it either.* When the unbelievers decide together not to pay any attention whatever to our do-as-we-say-and-not-as-we-do shtick, one must acknowledge that they kind of have a point.

Haven't they?

CHAPTER TWO

Restoring Sexism: The Lost Virtue

So the Bible is a sexist book, and that fact alone should make Christians want to acknowledge that sexism has to be a virtue. And because the Bible has been assiduously ignored when it comes to these matters for lo, these many years, this should make us realize that it is also a *lost* virtue. Therefore it must be renewed, or restored, or recovered, or perhaps even reupholstered. But how?

This is a Football

A story is told, and is perhaps apocryphal, about Vince Lombardi talking to his players after they had gotten badly beaten one time. "Men," he said, "It is time for us to get back to the fundamentals." And holding up the ball, he said, "*This* is a football."

When it comes to the optimal relationship between the sexes, I think we are pretty much at that point. Actually I mean that we are way *past* that point. What if the football identifies as six-year-old Asian girl? About the only thing the football couldn't identify as would be a Brooklyn rabbi, and that is because a pigskin isn't kosher, although there is reason to believe that we will soon overcome obstacles like that. But we are starting to stray from the point.

As we have now established that this is November, let me get back to the point and just say it. We have all been snookered. Sexism is certainly a sin against the gods of egalitarianism, but those gods are not gods at all. They are rather little wisps of aspirational fog floating off the sewage lagoon of late-stage secularism, and so we have no reason to feel bad about committing any such "sins." If they are not gods at all, then sins against their commandments are not sins at all.

The living God has given us His Word, and nowhere in that Word does it say that sexism is a sin against Him. That means it is not a sin at all. In fact, various things that our culture defines as sexist are enshrined as virtues in Scripture, and this means that Christians should stop their furtive glancing from side to side, and simply acknowledge that it is high time for us to recover the lost virtue of sexism.

But what would such a recovery look like? How might we recover our sexist heritage? How shall we know when we have recovered it? The heart and soul of a restored sexism is to recognize that God created men and women with different natures, and has commanded us to recognize those *natures* as different, and to treat men and women differently simply because they *are* men and women respectively.

There. I said it.

A Primer on Boys and Girls

Boys and girls are different. Men and women are different. The differences are not superficial or accidental, but rather are profound, extending from the tops of their heads down to the soles of their boots, or flats, as the case may be. The differences between them affect everything, and are found in virtually every aspect of their lives. Men and women both have ten toes, and men and women both have two kidneys, but that is about it.

Healthy cultures *budget* for these differences. Healthy cultures train boys and girls in terms of them. Boys are taught that they need to learn how to "do this" because they are boys. Girls are trained to do "certain things" because they are girls. Not only is sexism a virtue, but so is stereotyping!

I want to interrupt the proceedings in order to remind everybody that this is No Quarter November, and not No Kidding November. In other words, I am not skylarking here, but rather making a serious point. Well, actually, I am skylarking a little bit, but that doesn't affect the seriousness of the point.

What's at Stake

Up to this point, I dare say that quite a few conservatives are cheering me on in all such observations because they are currently being appalled by the androgynous end game—they are horrified by the insanities surrounding restrooms, and showers, and bio-males competing against girls, and all that kind of thing. And of course, I am against all of that too.

But you can't dial these things back "a little bit." If the culture has gone insane, you can't call it a great reformation when you get it back to almost insane.

To make this point a little bit clearer, I am not just talking about Bruno not being able to shower with the junior high girls. I am also talking about women not being able to go to the Naval Academy or West Point. And I am saying that they shouldn't be allowed to apply simply because they are female. No other reason is needed.

Women are not supposed to be warriors, and so we shouldn't be training them to be warriors (Deut. 22:5). And I know that there will be numerous conservatives, and you can supply your own scare quotes there, who will be upset by this. And it is that kind of conservative who is the problem. This is the kind of conservative who never conserves anything except the most recent progressive achievements. After women were introduced into combat roles, it took Fox News about five minutes to start saluting our "brave men and women in uniform." And they also, without even blinking, routinely show footage of service members returning from deployment in such a way as to surprise their family members, you know, those heartstrings videos, and they make no distinction whatever between men returning from war and women returning from war. Here's Mom, back from Afghanistan. If that doesn't make you sick and angry, then you are an essential part of the problem.

The Mirror of Nature

Upon occasion traditionalist conservatives will make an argument from nature, and it is an argument that resonates with those who still have some common sense hidden away in the basement. Last year when the federal government was engaged in that massive push, that big common sense buy-back, there were many—I have it on reliable authority—who ignored the federal diktat and who have kept quite a bit of unregistered common sense in their possession.

And this is why appeals to nature work for many people. They still use their common sense. But appeals to nature don't work with others, and so I want to walk through something here. How should we learn from nature?

Female robins build the nest, and male robins—when it comes to nest building—just horse around, helping only occasionally. If you spot a robin building a nest, the chances are excellent to outstanding that you are watching the female. And the chances are even better that "the patriarchy" had nothing to do with this arrangement. The female robin is not trapped in stereotypes derived from the 1950s. The female robin was not indoctrinated by the Victorians. That bird is simply doing *what it is her nature* to do.

Now if you started fuming to yourself over this illustration, then it appears to me that you have fallen into my trap. You were saying to yourself that you could go out into nature also, and you could find mother spiders that eat their young, or find female praying mantises that bite off the male's head while they are mating, and which consume the body later, or you could go out and find the occasional gay penguin. You can't just look at nature, they say condescendingly, and derive ethical norms.

Speaking of the gay penguin thing, I find that whole operation to be gay. Wearing those shiny little tuxes, and walking funny that way, and so what did you expect? But I digress.

Here is the trap that I mentioned earlier. We tend to think that "learning from nature" means watching things that go on in nature, and then using that to justify us doing the same thing in our own lives. If we can find it in a BBC nature doc, then we get to do it ourselves. But that is not reading nature; that is rather a pronounced form of natural illiteracy. That is not how nature is to be read at all. Otherwise, the objection mentioned above would have a point.

So my point was not that women should watch a female robin building her nest and take that as authoritative instruction from the "way things are," an authoritative word that requires her to paint the nursery and to hang the curtains. Not at all. If we were simply to imitate what the robins do, there is no good answer when someone asks why you aren't imitating the praying mantis instead. How would we respond to a man who joined the Shriners simply because he saw a male peacock at the zoo?

No, not at all. A man and woman watching a female robin build her nest should rather think something like this to themselves. "Look at that. *Creatures have natures.* Look at her nature there. I wonder what my nature is."

We do not look at nature from outside it. We do not observe nature as denatured individual observers. We are not standing on a balcony that overlooks the whole of nature, from which we see things that we may or may not adapt to our own condition. We are not natureless creatures out shopping for ways to invent ourselves. We don't get to invent ourselves. Our roles are assigned to us at conception.

If you were a male when you were conceived, this means that (at that moment) God was assigning to you the duties of provision and protection. If you were a female when conceived, you were being assigned the duties bearing children and nurturing them. And making the sandwiches.

We have questions. When there is an odd noise in the basement in the middle of the night, which one should go check? God wants the one with the XY chromosomes to go check. When dinner needs to be prepared, who is responsible to do that? Of course, the one with XX chromosomes should do that. Who should take out the garbage? XY. Who should go to war? XY. Who should learn to knit and cross stitch? XX.

A wail goes up over the land. These commandments are not to be borne. How can we be expected to bear it? Are there no exceptions, *no* qualifications? Well, not in November anyway.

The accusation comes. You would turn back the clock. You would once again trap women in the miserable condition they suffered in the 50s, the condition from which feminism liberated them. No, I am afraid you have misidentified where all the misery actually is.

Eggs Are Expensive, Sperm is Cheap

The title of this short section is taken from a book of the same name, a book[1] filled with bracing observations that are no doubt illegal in the author's home state of Maryland. And if you go to Amazon to buy it, you will discover that not only are eggs expensive, but so are copies of this book. I am just giving credit where it is due.

We human beings have natures. So when we disobey the requirements of Scripture that God gave to us with regard to sex roles, we are also disobeying our own bodies. We are disobeying the basic creational desires that God Himself planted in us. Women who reject motherhood are not just rejecting a law from outside them. They are also rejecting the same law that arises within them—which is why feminists are so hard, brittle, angry, and miserable. They are having to fight this war on multiple fronts.

When men abandon their responsibility to provide and protect, when they slouch into irresponsibility, they too are miserable. What are men *for?* Because eggs are expensive and sperm is cheap, men are expendable. But it is the glory of men to expend themselves on behalf of others. Expendable is not the same thing as optional. Men are necessary, because it is necessary to have protectors who are

1, Greg Krehbiel, *Eggs are Expensive, Sperm is Cheap: 50 Politically Incorrect Thoughts for Men* (Laurel, MD: Crowhill Publishing, 2014).

expendable. This is why sacrifice is at the heart of the code of any true man of honor.

One Last Thing

Some purists might not like the fact that I reasoned from nature and not from Scripture. But I reasoned from nature and not from Scripture because Scripture teaches us that on such matters we should reason from nature.

> For this cause God gave them up unto vile affections: for even their women did change *the natural use* into that which is *against nature*: And likewise also the men, leaving *the natural use* of the woman, burned in their lust one toward another; men with men working that which is unseemly, and receiving in themselves that recompence of their error which was meet. (Rom. 1:26-27)

> Doth not even *nature itself* teach you, that, if a man have long hair, it is a shame unto him? (1 Cor. 11:14)

> For the man is not of the woman; but the woman of the man. Neither was the man created for the woman; but the woman for the man. (1 Cor. 11:8-9)

There's a lot more, but you get the picture. On this subject of role relationships, when we submit to the authority of God, an authority which He expressed everywhere, we find the dislocated limb put back into joint. We find that someone turned the lens, and everything comes into focus. We find that we have sharpened the saw, and now it cuts.

We find that we were designed to walk upright and not on all fours, and it is such a relief to do it this way.

CHAPTER THREE

A Word in Defense of Rosaria, If I May

So the first order of business is perhaps a bit of background. Rosaria Butterfield recently gave an interview,[2] and in the course of that talk she gave us all an insight, and as is the case with many such insights, there was a pointy end to it. Someone then took that insight from the interview and tweeted it out to what was supposed to be a welcoming and friendly cyber-world. My friend Toby Sumpter retweeted that, and got what can only be described as A Reaction.

Here is what Rosaria said:

> Gay Christianity is a different religion. I'm not standing in
> the same forest with Greg Johnson and Wes Hill and Nate

2. "Interview with Dr. Rosaria Butterfield - From Victim to Guest: Sexuality, Intersectionality, and Hospitality," *Abounding Grace Radio Broadcast*, July 26, 2019, https://www.agradio.org/resource/interview-with-dr-rosaria-butterfield-from-victim-to-guest-sexuality-intersectionality-and-hospitality.

Collins looking at different angles of the trees, I'm in a different forest altogether.

This caused no small amount of official consternation, with all kinds of people calling upon Rosaria to repent of her slanderous evaluation of Johnson, Hill, and Collins. There has been, in short, a hubbub, a set-to, a fracas, an imbroglio, a brawl, a complication, an embroilment, a soap opera. And, as Toby Sumpter observed, the reactions ranged from a measured tutt-tutting to full-on meltdowns.[3]

So as I was reflecting on this statement from Rosaria, and I was jotting down some notes for this post, one of the things that occurred to me was how faithfully Rosaria was following in the footsteps of J. Gresham Machen. This is basically what he was arguing in his magisterial *Christianity and Liberalism*. Then I listened to the interview, and one of the first things that astute interviewer said was that this reminded him of J. Gresham Machen. On point and amen.

The point of Machen's book was to show that the Spirit of Christ and the spirit of liberalism were not the same spirit. They came from different places entirely, and they were going to different places entirely.

In a train station, it is possible for two trains to be lined up right alongside one another, looking for all the world like they are in perfect fellowship, one with another. But one train came from City A and is going to City B, while the other train came from City C and is going to City D. The superficial observer might look at the trains and the parallel tracks, sitting in alignment right there, and proclaim behold how good and how pleasant it is when the locomotives of harmony rest upon the true steel tracks of ecumenicity. But other observers—like Rosaria for instance—know how to read train schedules.

3. "Rosaria & Revoice in a 48hr. Petri Dish," November 4, 2019, https://www.tobyjsumpter.com/rosaria-revoice-in-a-48hr-petri-dish/.

Meanwhile, the kind-hearted fellow who likes to reason that "we are all saying the same thing here, really" is going to wind up spending a rainy weekend in Pittsburg instead of that sunny getaway to Ft. Lauderdale that his wife was so looking forward to.

In her remarks in the remainder of that interview, it became apparent that Rosaria's echoing of Machen was no accident. She was making a deliberate, sensible, measured, thoughtful case, just as Machen had, but these days deliberate, sensible, measured, and thoughtful engagement doesn't get you very far in the upper echelons of Presbyterian influence. Not that it ever did.

> A terrible crisis unquestionably has arisen in the Church. In the ministry of evangelical churches are to be found hosts of those who reject the gospel of Christ. By the equivocal use of traditional phrases, by the representation of differences of opinion as though they were only differences about the interpretation of the Bible, entrance into the Church was secured for those who are hostile to *the very foundations of the faith*.[4]

The Authority of Indelible Gayness

So it would be best to state the principle involved right at the outset, before we get into the particulars.

We are talking about the authority of Scripture over against the pretended authority of our feelings. We are talking about the authority of God to define sin (whether original, indwelling, or remaining), and whether our feelings should have any kind of veto power over

---

4. *Christianity and Liberalism* (1923; Grand Rapids: William B. Eerdmans, 2009), 150, emphasis mine.

such definitions. And we are talking about the power of the blood of Christ to cleanse any sin whatever, whether or not the authority of our feelings has granted prior permission for any such cleansing.

And so here we are, many decades later, talking about the same basic thing that Machen was addressing.

> It is no wonder, then, that liberalism is totally different from Christianity, for the foundation is different. Christianity is founded upon the Bible. It bases upon the Bible both its thinking and its life. Liberalism on the other hand is founded upon the shifting emotions of sinful men.[5]

There you have it—founding everything on the shifting emotions of sinful men. Which is like playing Jenga with an overwrought and squirrely toddler on a water bed.

The folly of this approach is not altered when the content of those feelings change. That is precisely what the shifting emotions do—they act like a weather vane in a stiff and fluctuating breeze. A lunatic king on a throne might give many inconsistent orders, not all of them equally insane, but the basic problem remains—to wit, a lunatic king on the throne, coupled with the fact that everybody lets him stay there.

The central problem is the authority we have ceded to our feelings, regardless of what those feelings feel. Those feelings may be of indelible gayness, or a bad temper, or craving for strong drink, or a smug feeling of racial vainglory, or the deep need to molest little boys.

It matters not. In classical Reformed theology, all such feelings are nothing more than cross fodder. Any feelings we have that are

---

5. *Christianity and Liberalism*, 67.

contrary to the holiness of God are to be loathed and despised by us, and not to be worn as badges of distinction.

And thus, to be a gay Christian is to be, by definition, a hypocrite. The fact that you have a theology that carves out room for that particular hypocrisy does not fix anything. It wrecks everything.

Watersheds

The apostle Paul once taught us all that we were not supposed to spiral down into debates about dumb stuff, about food and wine and all that (Rom. 14:1). But then, in a monstrous inconsistency, one other time he initiated a brawl with a fellow apostle over something as ridiculous as the *seating* arrangements at the potluck at Antioch Memorial. Not only did he do this, but then he had the effrontery to actually taunt the assembled brethren, his fathers and brothers in Israel, by saying that he didn't care what the Missouri Presbytery had determined, or an angel from heaven for that matter, or the horse they both rode in on (Gal. 1:8).

There are times when the little things don't matter at all, and there are times when the little things carry *everything* with them. This is elementary.

The late Francis Schaeffer illustrated this by talking about snow six inches apart. What is six inches, except for no big deal? Right over there, to our right, that length is a trivial difference. But if that same six inches is moved over here, in order to straddle the Continental Divide, then snow from one end of the six inches is going to wind up in the Pacific Ocean and snow from the other end is going to wind up in the Gulf of Mexico.

And so the point I am making here is that Rosaria Butterfield knows where the Continental Divide is. The Arbiters of Amiable who lament the regrettable intrusion of "divisive language" do not.

Rosaria used to live right near this train station, being that she used to commute in and out of it every day, and she really does know how to read the train schedules. These Ninjas of Nice do not.

Lest anyone mistake my meaning here, Rosaria knows what she is talking about, and her critics most manifestly do not.

Anyone who tries to pretend that "insignificant" issues like this cannot represent momentous and Church-corrupting realities is giving you what Francis Turretin used to call—with that wry smile of his—the sunshine runaround.

I think it was Gibbon who once tried to represent the debate over *homoousia* and *homoiousia* as a world-shaking debate over that little biddy letter, *iota*—as though, were we to pursue his insightful approach for determining what matters, we would discover the debate between atheism and theism somehow just became a debate over the letter a. Sometimes the wisdom of this world just falls over, twitching violently, and does not need to be answered.

So of course this is no *tomayto/tomahto* thing. This is not a discussion on whether to baptize with heads upstream or heads downstream, or even in the river at all. Rosaria is exactly right. This is a different forest, the trees are all unfamiliar, and it is getting darker by the minute. And it won't be the kind of night that you can dance away.

Accommodating Mediocrities

So allow me to explain how public opinion is shifted on things like this, including public opinion as it functions within ecclesiastical bodies. Here is the basic structure of the thing, with ratios and percentage points varying, as the particular case may be.

On either end of the spectrum, you have a committed five to ten percent, made up of people who know what is going on. In our case, in these instances, we have the epistemologically self-conscious progressives on one end, and we have the epistemologically self-conscious conservatives on the other end. Each side knows what they are doing, and what the other side is likely to do in return. We understand each other pretty well. The remaining 80 to 90 percent is made up of—on the central issue in question—accommodating mediocrities.

These accommodating mediocrities could be conservative or liberal, and it doesn't really much matter. Either kind can be steered, one with blandishments and the other with threats. Depending on the situation and the caliber of leadership, that middle can be driven by the committed on either end. So when Machen lost his battle with the mainline Presbyterian Church, a good eighty percent of the ministers would have called themselves conservative and evangelical. What matters is that this big middle be both accommodating and mediocre.

"What is all the fuss?" they inquire. "All this about the letter a? We are going to tear apart the seamless garment of Christ over the letter a?"

Champions on one end, churls on the other, and chumps in the middle.

Inescapable Discipline

In the eyes of the PCA, a conservative is considered temperate when he thinks it a requirement of principle to put up with it whenever he is accused of intemperance, which is routinely.

All effective conservatives, no matter how temperate their demeanor, are regularly accused of intemperance, and the "good" conservatives are the ones who go along with this charade quietly.

You doubt what I say? Consider this measured, even, judicious,
calm, and loving presentation at the last PCA General Assembly by
Steve Warhurst. It was delivered late in the evening, going on mid-
night, and yet some guys with parliamentary nunchucks tried to shut
him down even then. And since that fifteen minutes of infamy, hun-
dreds of PCA ministers have signed a petition, apparently without any
sense of embarrassment, protesting the Inflammatory Outburst of
One Steven Warhurst. Go ahead. Watch the whole video. I dare you.[6]
He had the effrontery to read some passages from the epistle to the
Romans on the floor of General Assembly, a thing not to be borne.

Discipline is inescapable. No social organization can exist without it. So the only question is which group will be disciplined, not
whether there will be discipline. Because the PCA has in effect
declined to discipline the Revoice agitators, this necessarily means
that—whether they intended this outcome or not—they have committed themselves to the policy of disciplining people who oppose
Revoice. They are obligated now to deal with people who actually
believe what the Bible says about carnality carnivals like Revoice.
As Dylan put it in a moment of profound lucidity, channeling his
Rushdoony, you gotta serve somebody.

Inescapable. A refusal to discipline the wolves is in effect a decision to discipline shepherds who insist on identifying and fighting
the wolves.

Now if we hunted around for a feminine voice that was fully as
temperate and as calm and as kind as Warhurst's voice was, we would almost certainly settle on Rosaria. And because discipline is inescapable,

6. "Steven Warhurst Speech at 2019 PCA General Assembly," June 28, 2019, you-
tube.com/watch?v=BmYF5HN1pWQ&feature=emb_logo.

and because discipline is always applied *in terms of the actual issue*, and because the issue of temperate language or its apparent absence is not the issue AT ALL, the machinery of discipline is already warming up and starting to hum. Rosaria is not in the PCA, but if she were, there would no doubt be formal complaints already wending their way to the presbyterial filing cabinets of intersectional justice.

So think about this. Ponder it a bit. I will give you a minute if you like. Stare at the ceiling if it helps.

In the Revoice materials, their use of that LGBTQ+ plus sign declared, in the most thinly-veiled way possible, that pedophiles are sexual minorities too. If they are not to be considered a sexual minority, why aren't they, given the logic of the last few years? And if they are a sexual minority, then why do we not dispense with this coy + business? They were born this way, and cannot deny the sheer fact their desires. They can decline to act on those desires—for now, since that is the current line we are taking—meaning that their internal cesspool of yearning for the under-aged can be harnessed by the celibate but pedophilic Jesus follower, committed as he is to no actual touching. Nothing of any significance happened to the folks who are prepping us for gunk like that. Steven Warhurst read some Bible verses at General Assembly, and everybody lost their minds. A Petition of Stern Rebuke is called for, and even now is circulating.

I already knew that discipline was an inescapable concept, but it really is kind of a thrill to see it come to pass before your very eyes. "Look!" I cry. "Discipline is inescapable. Either the heterodox will be disciplined or the orthodox will be! See that?" And I admit that the reply thus far has been somewhat dispiriting. "*Wut?*"

Now the stated reason the squishy middle puts up with intemperate and inflammatory expressions from the Revoice gang—e.g. "queer treasure in the New Jerusalem" and "sexual minorities" and other such crap—is because they want to be *missional*. And thanks to Screwtape, what a fine word *that's* turned out to be! Missional must mean something like beaming winsomely at travesties. But nobody wants to be missional toward hardline conservatives.

Being missional means not saying anything off-putting that might put a kink in anyone's kink. The only thing that they feel constrained in the conscience to not tolerate is the rising Hydra-head of Legalism, that nefarious kind of works-righteousness that seeks to be obedient to what God says to do, the way He says to do it.

Already Gay in the PCA

So Warhurst is supposed to be intemperate in his language, and why? My guess would be that he quoted some Scripture that contained the word *vile* with reference to homosexual passions.

Rosaria is supposed to have transgressed a great boundary line of decorum by her recognition that to place certain sins outside the reach of the Lord's saving power is in effect a different gospel.

Now allow me to point something out. Somebody apparently needs to indicate that the sky is still blue, and so permit me.

Nobody could have been more judicious than Steven Warhurst in that presentation of his. And nobody in the country has a more established and compelling ethos when it comes to compassion and kindness extended to those trapped in homosexual confusions than Rosaria Butterfield has.

But that doesn't matter to the tone police. However, they are not really tone police, but rather tone trolls—as a brief glance at the twitter feed of any effective conservative will quickly demonstrate. They are the ones whose job it is to prevent and head off any articulate and effective opposition to the encroachments of the sexual revolution. Their task is simply to intimidate, which they try to do with exhortations about the tone that run along the lines of 'you-worthless-effin'-excuse-for-a-Christian-this-is-why-I-left-the-effin'-church!'" If you can't answer the arguments, then you can still make it stink. Speaking of tone . . .

Now when it comes to actual tone, some observers have said, for example, that I can be somewhat exuberant. I have occasionally used the gaudy metaphor. When November rolls around betimes, I have periodically said things that have furrowed the brows of some. At this great banquet of Reformed thought leaders that I managed to sneak into, I have from time to time thrown a dinner roll at the waiter carrying the champagne tray. This is acknowledged, although there is more to that story than one might suspect (Prov. 18:17), with one point of my defense being that it was a metaphorical dinner roll and a hypothetical waiter.

But all this is also beside the point. My voice is opposed the way it is because it is *effective*. Rosaria's is opposed because she is *effective*. That is our central offense, the central sin, and in the new order, it is the unforgivable sin. Voices of opposition are different because people are different, but the goals of the sexual revolution are constant and focused. And one of the goals of the sexual revolution is that of reserving the right to be triggered by absolutely anything or anybody. In David Cassidy's open letter of concern to Rosaria, for example, he mentioned a problem with her "shaming" use of humor.

Yeah, right. Rosaria Butterfield, jokester firebrand.

The Dhimmitude of Mammon

One of the reasons all this is working against us is because we are Americans who figured out ways to monetize everything. We have advertisers on our blogs, we have vendors at our conferences, and we have sponsors for our podcasts. Look at us go. But we have not yet figured out how to respond strategically when those supply lines are threatened, which they routinely are.

This is because there are plenty of merchants who are more than willing to cater to your conference, just so long as there is no controversy or trouble, but who are quickly spooked as soon as there is a sign of opposition. They are not against your cause, and were more than willing to serve it, just so long as the good old cash flow were not threatened.

So Mammon is not just a problem when people give way to the greasier forms of greed, sitting like Scrooge McDuck on a pile of gold coins. Mammon is a subtle god, and has more tricks than that. There are many individual Christians who are not individually greedy, but who are nevertheless vulnerable when Mammon puts the screws to their suppliers.

Let us say that somebody says a sensible something that goes viral, or publishes a book that explodes on the scene, or has a moment of courage like the one that put Jordan Peterson on the map. Depend upon it, the Wokestapo will swing immediately into action, and target all the relevant vendors, suppliers, and sponsors. We are now living in a cancel culture, and the woke within our ranks have no qualms whatever about "deplatforming" the opposition.

More than a few conservatives would be stalwart in a straight up debate, and would defend their own position ably. But they have no idea what to do when the enemy bombs their supply lines.

We have plenty of foot soldiers, and courageous ones too. We have many able colonels. What we need are some generals. Not parade ground generals, *generals*.

What It Purports to Be, and What It Actually Smells Like

The enlightened progressives say they are giving us a Yankee Candle with traces of aromatic rosemary, but what we wound up with was a small Mason jar filled with rancid pig grease, and a smoky trail of black smudge crawling slowly around the living room. I am not picking up on any rosemary at all.

Progressives think they are inviting us to an opportunity to share our deepest feelings and concerns, but then it somehow always turns into a North Vietnamese Self-Criticism Session.

Regardless, a number of us see exactly what is going on, and some of that number are willing to say so. Preeminent among those who see and understand the play that is being run on us is Rosaria Butterfield. She is a woman of kindness and courage, and she has something important to say. Let us agree together—shall we?—to hear the lady out. To accuse her of slander when she simply points out what should have been obvious to us is what observers in another time would have called the Limit. To accuse her of slander is, frankly speaking, an audacious move. Let's make sure it is a move that doesn't work.

"What is today a matter of academic speculation begins tomorrow to move armies and pull down empires."[7]

---

7. "Christianity and Culture," in *Princeton Theological Review* 11 (1913): 6.

CHAPTER FOUR

So Many Bowls of Tapioca at Room Temperature

I believe that perhaps I should start with the least controversial part of my thesis here today, which is that a good deal of what we see around us in today's culture is the result of a vast conspiracy calculated to make it possible for beta males to get laid. Thus far we agree? Perhaps I will return to this point later.

Character or Personality?

Let us begin with the observation that in the short term character costs and personality pays. But nevertheless both have a way of winding up in leadership positions somehow. Character is the slow and old school way of approaching it, the approach which pays its dues, while personality simpers its way to the top, shucking and jiving as it goes, glad-handing, sandpapering the hard edges, and of course networking.

In short, character climbs while personality floats. While every society gets the leadership it deserves—a thought which should be chilling to every loyal American who contemplates the current impeachment proceedings—the means for getting the leadership it deserves varies from one culture to another. Every society rewards certain behaviors and penalizes others. In our day, we are rewarding the floaters and penalizing the climbers.

Just as America has turned away from leaders through character, and toward leaders with personalities, so also has the evangelical Church done the same thing. Far from providing a true spiritual counterculture, we have adopted the demented view that there isn't anything the world can do that will not result in an evangelical knock-off. The deep driver of this is our imitation of the personality ethic instead of the character ethic. The personality ethic is all flash and show, and so everything has got to be on the surface. And if everything is on the surface, we cannot be shocked and dismayed at the superficial consequences.

Resultant examples range from the trivial to the tragically absurd. If the Calvin Klein logo is hot, we can reverse engineer our own Christ the King logo that looks just like it. And on the tragic end, if the world decides to plunge into the madness of woke, there we are, right on schedule. We decide, mysteriously, to strive for that holy grail of liberalism, the ultimate irrelevance of relevance. This is why Eric Mason calling for a woke Church ought to strike us the same way that the band Stryper did back in the eighties.

We can also see this in the ubiquity of that loathsome word *celebrities*. Life coaches, rock stars, actresses, authors, agents, marketers, publicists—you name it, we got it.

About the only place where a celebrity is genuinely useless is on the field of battle. And guess where we are right now? Right. On the threshold of battle.

But Battles Still Happen Anyway

The virtues that seemed so dispensable during extended times of peace are suddenly in high demand when danger starts to appear. All of a sudden, the celebrity culture which had us so entranced—here in the evangelical ghetto of Vanity Fair—seems kind of lame. It had been so easy to sneer at heroics when heroics seemed unnecessary and passé. It had been the matter of a moment to dismiss the dark warnings of those who—for some reason—liked to issue dark warnings.

> And the king of Israel said unto Jehoshaphat, There is yet one man, Micaiah the son of Imlah, by whom we may inquire of the LORD: but I hate him; for he doth not prophesy good concerning me, but evil. And Jehoshaphat said, Let not the king say so. (1 Kgs. 22:8)

Yeah. Let not the king say so. Let not the parade ground generals, quasi-celebrities in their own right, at least when there are no wars in sight, grumble too much about the arrival of actual soldiers. They may actually be needed.

In short, our evangelical establishment has been like the merchants of Dale, and the outsiders are like Bard, grim and unbending, but a lot more useful when it comes to killing dragons than the Dale Chamber of Commerce would be.

We are now standing on the edge of the field of battle, and the distant howitzers have begun to speak in that throaty way of theirs, and we are having trouble arranging our celebrities in a reasonable order. Nothing is working out, and a bunch of them already want to leave. I mean, we already lost Josh Harris. What are we going to *do*?

Thus we have a generation of leaders who do not know how to fight, wouldn't want to if they did know how to, and who are fully prepared to vilify anyone who suggests that a fight might be in order.

The fighting spirit which is the screaming need of the hour is disdained. Our leadership acts like so many bowls of tapioca at room temperature. They have about as much courage as could be carved out of a peeled and overripe banana. The dauntlessness that we are now in desperate need of is a dauntlessness that has disappeared with the whistling wind. We are living in a post-dauntless era. The pluck that used to be admired back when your great-grandparents were tots is the kind of demeanor that is admired no more. The spunk that used to characterize our people is a spunk that has been largely despunkified.

But Lewis said it well when he said that courage is not so much a separate virtue as it is the testing point of all the virtues.[8]

Intelligent Warriors

But the fighting spirit is not just a spirit that is thoughtless, pugnacious, or belligerent. The kind of fighting spirit I am talking about is not the kind that gets into random bar fights. I am talking about a fighting Spirit, actually. Think of Othniel.

---

8. *The Screwtape Letters* (1942; New York: HarperCollins, 2001), 161

> And the Spirit of the LORD came upon him, and he judged Israel,
> *and went out to war.* and the LORD delivered Chushan-rishathaim
> king of Mesopotamia into his hand; and his hand prevailed
> against Chushan-rishathaim. (Judg. 3:10, emphasis added)

This kind of fighting spirit *is intelligent.* It sees what is going on. It identifies how the enemy has arranged his troops. It sees and understands.

So who or what is the culprit in all of this? There are many contributing factors, and books could be written about each one of them. But I want to single out what I believe to be the central villain of the piece. We must see where the problem is, we must plead for the Holy Spirit to grant us boldness, and we must fight in that boldness.

Where is the problem? Why do we live in a time when people can seriously maintain—without being hooted from the stage—that there are no differences between men and women, between virginity and experience, between courage and cowardice, between freedom and slavery, between immigration and collapsed borders, between one tribe and another, between savings and debt, between the authority of the Constitution and the authority of courts, and so on? Why does Western Culture now look like a watercolor that somebody left out in the rain?

A reformation and revival would teach us how to paint with oils again.

We no longer believe that things have fixed *essences;* we no longer think that creatures have *natures* contained within boundaries and edges. Because of that, we are in a bad epistemological jam, and we cannot get out of it by ourselves. We—all together—need to call upon Jesus, who will bring us back to His Father (and at the same time back to our senses). His Father is the one who made Heaven and earth, and when He made Heaven and earth, He filled it full of discrete and bounded things. And these discrete and bounded things had and have essential natures. They were not just *shaped* to look like something, but rather were given the internal *essence* of those things.

So a woman is not just matter shaped like a woman—she is essentially a woman. All the way through. The same goes for a boy, and so on down the entire list. A boy does not just look like a boy. He has the nature of a boy. You may say I'm a dreamer, but I'm not the only one . . .

We are in a battle, therefore, between a world made out of *social constructs* and the world made out of *created essences*. If the world around us is the former, then we have the authority and power to do all the dumb stuff we are currently attempting. If the world around us is the latter, then this explains why all these dumb attempts are so staggeringly lame. Which they really are.

In the world they think they are in, a sex-change operation is simply rearranging the furniture. In the world they are actually in, a sex-change operation is more like putting lipstick on a camel and calling it *séduisante*. Without an essential nature, the core of everything has been hollowed out, and this means that the meaning of the surfaces is up for grabs. So when we Christians say that a man cannot just declare himself to be a woman, that he is a man all the way through, this makes no sense to those who have been catechized in the belief that there is no such thing as a fixed and given nature. But returning to the point made earlier, we are well past the point where it will be sufficient to simply *say* that we have created natures.

Some of us, those who were created for fighting and assigned by God to the fight, must actually fight. It is not enough to look like a warrior. It has to go clean through.

CHAPTER FIVE

Gallio Cared for None of These Things

In an earlier NQN post, I said that to be a gay Christian was to be a hypocrite, by definition. What could be the basis for saying things like that? The guy who says that he is a gay Christian, although committed to remaining celibate, is a hypocrite? And he is a hypocrite because he doesn't formulate it precisely the way I said he should, which is to say that he is a Christian who experiences gay temptations? Right. *Exactly so.*

In short, a gay Christian is a hypocrite while a Christian *seeking to mortify/fight/resist* his gay temptations is not? Correct. Aside from the problems associated with the history of the word *gay*, that summary is good enough.

For some this is an inside baseball debate between American League fans and National League fans debating the value of a designated hitter. But it is not that kind of debate at all.

Or take a scriptural example. The casual observer might be forgiven if he thought to himself that everybody might want to adopt the posture of Gallio. "But if it be a question of words and names, and of your law, look ye to it; for I will be no judge of such matters" (Acts 18:15). Deal me out, in other words.

And this is why you can't. This is why you have to deal with this issue honestly. Those who do not deal with it honestly will not inherit the kingdom of Heaven (1 Cor. 6:9-11; Gal. 5:19-21).

What the Issue is Not

The issue is not whether there can be such a thing as a besetting sin, or a recurring sin, or remaining sin that travels in predictable patterns. Christians are never to be dismissed as hypocrites simply because of a struggle with remaining sin. And this is not affected by what the sin might be. This is the case no matter how many times the sin pops up in their life. The issue is not the repented sin in question, but rather the *unrepented* sin that is actually the real question.

So the charge of hypocrisy comes from the act of naming oneself in an ungodly way, with a name that contradicts the name given in one's baptism. The hypocrisy lies in the fact of taking the white stone upon which your new name was inscribed (Rev. 2:17) and taking it down to a tattoo parlor to see if you can't get them to draw a lithesome little guy in a Speedo on it. A stunt like that might indicate that what you have isn't that white stone after all. The children of Israel were told to bind the law of God to their foreheads or right hands (Deut. 6:8). They were not told to bind there the name of the Canaanite nation that held the greatest allure for them. Which of them do you have the strongest yearnings to join? Nobody was allowed to be a Canaanite-attracted Israelite. People did do that, but it was usually considered a problem.

The mark of the beast cannot be taken on the forehead or right hand (Rev. 13:16-17) because that is the place reserved for the holy law of God. This issue of gay Christianity is like many before it in the history of God's covenant people—there are those who want to offer the tiniest pinch of incense to the emperor, and the answer is as difficult as it is simple. *You may not.*

To make it simple and clear, and blunt enough for November, what I am saying is this: A Christian with such temptations may *not* identify himself as a gay Christian. He may, however, describe himself as a Christian who remains vulnerable to temptations of a same sex nature. The latter is simple honesty, and nobody should object to it.

And this is where a number of people think we are splitting the hair lengthwise, into four or more strands. The fact that it strikes us this way is a testament to just how powerful the homosexual propaganda barrage has been, even among Christians. We have been pounded with this lying message six ways from Sunday, and it turns out that being pounded with a big lie works, regardless of how outrageous the lie is.

Why Doesn't This Work With Other Sins?

To show that we are not hair-splitting, not even a little bit, let us try this out with other sins, shall we?

Suppose you had a man in your fellowship, married for thirty years, and with five kids. He is a deacon in your church, and up until this hypothetical incident I am about to describe, well respected in the church. One day, he starts identifying himself, and quite publicly, as a porn-attracted Christian. This causes no small consternation in the church, not to mention with his wife, but that conversation happened mostly off-site. But during sharing times at the prayer meeting, say, he would say, "Speaking as a porn-attracted Christian myself . . . ."

He agrees with everybody that he ought not to look at porn, and that for the most part he doesn't. But, he says, "I feel that tug constantly. When something pops up on my screen, it takes everything I've got to look away."

"I have come to realize," he says sadly, "that this is just a fact about me that I must be willing to accept. This is just the way I will be until I die—a porn-attracted Christian. And when all the sinful dross associated with this sensibility has been cleansed away, I look forward to the time when my cleansed porn-attractions will be enabled by grace to bring something of true value into the New Jerusalem."

But sin is not some beautiful thing that needs to have the sin wiped off of it. A turd is what it is all the way through.

So all God's people said *ummmm*. Now nothing will be served by disputing with this guy over whether or not he is porn-attracted. Of *course* he is. Welcome to earth, champ. Have you been here long?

The main issue is not that *tug* he is *de*scribing. The main issue is the *name* he is *a*scribing. The issue is not the fact of temptations to look at porn. As John Owen put it, a man should not think he makes any progress in godliness if he does not walk daily over the bellies of his lusts. That part is uncontroversial.

Corrupt Naming

Our quarrel is not with the fact of his temptations, but rather with his theology of those temptations. *That is where the trouble is.* A man can have a recurring temptation and not be a hypocrite. We pray for him because we all pray for one another. If it comes to that, absolutely all of us are in the same boat. But when he crowns himself with the name of that sin and puts that unholy name next to the holy name of Christ, he is a hypocrite. If he were to identify himself as a thieving Christian, or reviling Christian, or road-rage Christian, or pedophile Christian, he would have done something appalling. When he identifies himself as a gay Christian, he has done the same appalling thing.

The only reason it doesn't seem appalling to us is because we have been conditioned to accept it. But bringing gay sensibilities into the presence of the God of our holy and new Jerusalem should be as unthinkable as asking Moses to offer up a pig on the altar of some high place borrowed from the Moabites.

Christ is at war with all sin, and all sin is at war with Christ. They are both seeking to occupy the same position or level in the life of the believer, and they both make total claims. Those claims are necessarily inconsistent because no man can serve two masters (Matt. 6:24; Luke 16:13).

> Know ye not that the unrighteous shall not inherit the kingdom of God? Be not deceived: neither fornicators, nor idolaters, nor adulterers, nor effeminate, nor abusers of themselves with mankind, Nor thieves, nor covetous, nor drunkards, nor revilers, nor extortioners, shall inherit the kingdom of God. And such were some of you: but ye are washed, but ye are

> sanctified, but ye are justified in the name of the Lord Jesus,
> and by the Spirit of our God. (1 Cor. 6:9–11)

Not one of those tawdry items on that list can be turned into an acceptable adjective for any one of God's saints. It is spiritually oxymoronic to try—a dirty holy one. A holy one can fall and get dirty, but it is so inconsistent that he cries out to his Father for cleansing (1 John 1:9). But as soon as he makes his peace with the dirt, as soon as he tries to incorporate whatever his precious is into the name by which he was called, he has crossed a deadly line. And he who is filthy, let him be filthy still (Rev. 22:11).

What about other adjectives then? A man can be an American Christian or a Korean Christian because those identifiers are not inconsistent with each other. They occupy different levels on the identity scale, and thus they are not at war. Thus a man can be a baseball-playing Christian, or a guitar-playing Christian, or a sushi cook Christian. Sure. They are on different levels, provided no idolatry is involved.

And yes, I believe the first fatal step in this downgrade was taken some time ago in our approach to the treatment of alcoholics. Can a man be an alcoholic Christian? I would argue *no*. A man can be a Christian whose temptations revolve around the abuse of alcohol, but who is he? His identity is Christ, and only Christ.

Conclusion

We are defined by our Savior, and never by that which we were saved from. Our identity is Christ, and our identity is in Christ alone. Our name of Christian is grounded in Christ, plus nothing else and no one else. We are called Christians, and because Christ fills all Heaven and earth there is no room there for any supplementary adjectives—and especially adjectives which challenge His power to cleanse and forgive.

You shall call His name Jesus because He will save His people from their sins (Matt. 1:21).

CHAPTER SIX

The Grace of White Privilege

I went back and forth in my mind about the title of this little thing. It came down to *intersectional privilege* or *white privilege*, even though I was going to make the same basic points either way. And so, naturally, I asked myself which one would be more inflammatory. *Ha ha*, he joked.

A Little DNA Data

Before getting to it, if I want to talk about my white privilege, the very first thing to do is to establish my *bona fides*. As a result of the intrepid work of our friends over at AncestryDNA.com, it appears that 63% of my stock was the result of various flirtatious mash ups, some of which were probably not a good idea *at all*, in Northern England, Wales, the Scottish lowlands, and Northern Ireland. Ireland and Scotland contributed a distinct 27%. Germanic Europe chipped in with 2%, and Norway weighed in with 8%—with a possible dollop coming from Iceland. *Iceland.* All of this is to acknowledge—as I hope I am doing frankly and without guile—that I am kind of white.

Let us be frank. I am almost as white as Elizabeth Warren's very high cheekbones. I am almost as white as Justin Trudeau's undercoat.

So much for the background facts. The difficulty arises when I indicate by various rhetorical devices (such as these pesky things here called *words*) that I refuse to feel bad about any of this. I have read my Bible multiple times and the only place where *anybody* felt bad about somebody being white was right after Aaron saw that Miriam had been turned as white as snow (Num. 12:10). But that had only happened to her because she had spoken out against Moses on account of the black Ethiopian lady he had married. I, on the other hand, have always thought it was kind of cool that Moses had married a Cushite, and so it has come to pass that the good Lord has not seen any need to make me look any more mid-winter Icelandic than I already do. And besides, most scholars agree that leprosy doesn't really count.

But here is why it is such a shame that intersectional analysis had not really been fully developed by the time of the Exodus, because both Miriam *and* Aaron had spoken out against Moses (Num. 12:1), and yet only Miriam got herself whitened. Is this not yet one more case of *male* privilege? If we consider the post-structural contributions of Germaine Fischer-Baine Tinkweiler, EdD, whose landmark work on the post-colonial female breast as both social construct *and* embodied intuition confirms this intersectional solution, it seems hard to deny.

And yet, we have to remember that intersectional analysis is still in its infancy and we have not completely settled on the appropriate weights and measures that go with things like birth order, sex, sexuality, race, looks, straight white teeth, class, and so on. For example, we don't even know if lesbianism comes in cubits or ephahs.

And it is kind of hard to know how to play *rock, paper, scissors* when you don't know what beats what.

The Central Offense Here

Okay. Enough with the horsing around. What is going to attract the ire of some in all of this is the fact that I freely acknowledge being (really) white, and in addition I grant that this comes with certain privileges that others don't have access to, and the harmonic conjunction of these two realities does not bother me at all. I don't feel guilty about *any* of it. I can swank around in this white epidermis all day long, and yet sleep like a baby. The whiteness and white privilege both go together, and even my *name* is Scottish.

Of course, honesty compels me to mention that this name—Douglas—means something along the lines of "out of the black swamp." This is, I don't mind saying, a little bit hurtful. One time I checked one of those spinner racks in a Christian store, the ones with little plaques with your name on it, along with the meaning of the name in question, and an associated verse. You know, really edifying stuff. I was curious with how they would manage "out of the black swamp," but I needn't have worried. The Christian merch industry was up to the challenge, and rendered my name as meaning "seeker of light," which is presumably what someone ensconced in a black swamp would be seeking. Or at least should be seeking. Where was I?

Right. I was not feeling bad about something that all the virtuous cis-lords in the land are currently insisting that I feel bad about. Virtually every campus in North America is ablaze with indignation over the unbearable whiteness of being, and which most certainly includes my contributions to it.

So as Francis Schaeffer might have asked, how then shall we be white?

Euro-centric Truth?

The central driving engine of all this current pomo madness is the idea that a commitment to fixed, objective truth is itself a Euro-Western form of racism and oppression. If I maintain that we have to consider the actual *facts* first, then I have given myself away as an oppressor. Only oppressors and colonial masters think like that. If I do not bow down before this current narrative, and if I do not festoon that narrative with whatever *convenient* facts may be ready at hand, while leaving any inconvenient facts in the box, then I have revealed myself to be a monster.

This is the world we now live in, but it does simplify things for thinking Christians somewhat. If the bad guys dismiss truth the way they do, then this means that they have sold themselves into the service of the lie. Dismissing truth is a grand identifier. It is a uniform.

Jesus is the Truth, and because He is the Truth, we live in a world where truths matter, all truths, and all the way down. Truth really is fixed, objective, normative, unbudgeable, and absolute. All those who assail the reality of objective truth have therefore hoisted their dirty mendacity flag, revealing them to be loyal servants of the lie.

So to traffic in the tropes of multiculturalism, diversity, wokeness, social justice, intersectionality, feminism, critical theory, socialism, cultural Marxism, postmodernism, or climate change means one of two things. Either you are a liar peddling lies, or you are a chump peddling lies. That's it. No more options are actually available.

Before racial reconciliation can be accomplished, we have to understand that ethnic tensions can only be resolved in the world God made and through the cross Christ died on. Nothing whatever is going to be accomplished by appointing a bunch of commies to the editorial boards of all of our dictionaries. So whiteness is a problem, is it? Before we talk about that, what world are we in? The world God made, with sin defined by Him? Or the world you are trying to make, with all sin defined by you?

If the latter, then perhaps you will pardon me if I just walk away.

The Politics of Privilege Explained

In the world they are trying to construct, race (and sex, and everything else) is merely a social construct, which is kind of like attempting to build an obelisk the size of the Washington Monument out of *papier mâché*. All it has to do is rain a couple of times and their future glory will sink down into a sodden mass, a great pile of former grandeur. No doubt its failure will be attributed to the secret machinations and plots of the capitalists.

In the world God actually made, the question of white or black is a biological fact, *and not a religio-political identity*. In the world they desire to build with their epistemic *papier mâché*, the correct religio-political identity is everything and trumps every creational fact.

We Christians believe that Jesus is Lord, and so it is that His Word governs all, and determines the nature of things. These secularists believe that their burgeoning state is lord, and so it is that its word (aka *their* word) should govern all, and determine the nature of things, which is—as they have now solemnly decreed—fluid. Their death grip on the dictionary editorial decisions is, however, not at all fluid.

The world is always governed by the god of the system, of necessity, and so this lunatic cultural episode we are all witnessing should be tagged for what it is, that is to say, a demented effrontery. The god of their system is directly challenging the God who dwells in unapproachable light.

> I will ascend into heaven, I will exalt my throne above the stars of God: I will sit also upon the mount of the congregation, in the sides of the north: I will ascend above the heights of the clouds; I will be like the most High. (Is. 14:13–14)

Yeah. Been tried before.

White Black People

If you doubt what I say, why are Clarence Thomas and Thomas Sowell not generally hailed as black exemplars? The answer is simple, if you consider it for more than ten minutes. It is because they are not *really* black. Black is now a religio-political identity, and this idolatrous approach to politics requires that it swallow up everything. They are not black for the same reason that Margaret Thatcher was not a woman. Why isn't anybody in the racial reconciliation crowd reaching out to Voddie Baucham?

Black and *woman* and *gay* and so on have been transformed into political favors to be handed out to political favorites. The fact that the first two are creational gifts and the third is a sexual perversion doesn't change anything about the game that is being played. When Peter Thiel endorsed Trump, Thiel being that man who said at the Republican convention that he was "proud to be gay" to whoops and cheers, he was stripped by the progressives of his "status" as a gay man. It turns out that just about everybody is confused, especially Republicans.

This is why a black conservative is, in *their* world, an oxymoron. They are in charge of genuine blackness™—and black conservatives don't have it. They are the arbiters of true womanhood™—and a pro-life woman is, in their minds, a sexual heretic and this is why she has to be summarily excommunicated. Rachel Dolezal, with the wrong color but the right opinions, was far more black than Clarence Thomas; he the one with the right color and wrong opinions.

What matters to them is not what God did, but what they say. What matters to them is not skin color considered as a creational reality. The only thing they care about is their orthodoxy (defined as them getting their way, no matter what).

All of this, from front to back, top to bottom, side to side, is a simple and straightforward power play. And they are running this power play on a traditional establishment that doesn't even know how to stop a toddler pitching a fit in a restaurant. Still less do they know how to stop a million antifa toddlers, from pitching the same kind of fit.

Zero Sum Envy

The spiritual rot that is driving all of this is the crushing sin of envy. Privilege (perceived or real) is always resented by the envious, and they are the only ones who resent it. Privilege is never resented by the grateful, by the contented, by the saints of God.

If God has blessed someone else with more smarts, then God bless him. If God has blessed her with better looks, then may God continue to bless her. If God has blessed him with wealth and favor, it sounds like something straight out of the book of Deuteronomy.

When the rich steal from the poor, or defraud them, the problem is the stealing (Jas. 5:4-5). The problem is not the mere fact of income inequality. The problem is the *stealing*.

> A stone is heavy, and the sand weighty; but a fool's wrath is heavier than them both. Wrath is cruel, and anger is outrageous; but who is able to stand before envy? (Prov. 27:3–4)

The envious simply assume that if there is any difference at all, then an offense has necessarily been committed. This is why the mere existence of any kind of privilege is an affront to them. They assume that every good in the world is apportioned in a zero sum game, meaning that if one person has more, then that means the others have less because of the guy who has more. But this is not the way God dispenses blessings.

In a world free of envy, one person getting a bigger slice of pie does not necessitate others getting a smaller piece because in a world free of envy, the pie grows. What would you rather? A smaller fraction of a huge pie or a huge fraction of a teeny pie? But enough about socialism.

Parents who love each other and stay together are imparting unbelievable privileges to their children. Parents who read to their children are doing the same. Parents who take their kids to the orthodontist are also privilege-mongers. Parents who provide their kids with warmth, food, security, and education are strewing privilege out of a sack with both hands. How can privilege be evil when God commands parents to give so much of it to their children?

So the best way to bequeath privilege to your children is to ensure that they grow up in a home free from envy. And if they grow up in a home where envy is recognized for the soul-destroying sin that it is, then this is also the best way to equip them to deal with a world that is crammed full of envy, a world that runs on envy. Growing up in an envy-free home is the best way to build up an immune system against this pandemic of ulcerated sores that the world likes to call social justice.

A world full of envy cannot deal with Christians who laugh effortlessly.

A Small Gallimaufry of Observations

White privilege is supposed to be everywhere and in everything, like the frogs of Egypt. Only nobody can see them, so they are the invisible frogs of Egypt. In fact, we only know there are there because the priests of Egypt have told us about them. But why are you listening to the priests of Egypt?

White privilege is supposed to be this insidious thing that becomes deadly if denied. In other words, if you deny that you are guilty of white privilege, in the senses ascribed to you, then they instantly up the ante because they think their culture is in peril. This is why they turn you into a white supremacist, and they do that by simply declaring you to be one.

The ease with which numerous online commenters hurl accusations of white supremacy around—let us call them "click bait lies"—shows how this racism inflation works. Racism is no longer the sin they are trying to rid us of. Rather, charges of racism is the discipline that is applied whenever anybody who is guilty of any of the other sins they have made up.

This is not a white/black thing, but it illustrates what is being done to the word *privilege*. When the amphibious landing craft were approaching Normandy beach, they were all exclusively filled with young males, holding their guns nervously, and our generation has taken to calling this kind of thing male privilege. I grant that there was privilege involved, but submit that according to this calculus, the privilege was elsewhere.

This is how we know we are dealing with the apostles and priests of a new religion, a religion entirely distinct from the Christian faith. They are laying sovereign claim *over every word in the dictionary*, and they have the impudence to believe they are going to pull it off.

In the grip of this folly, they claim that *they* are the intelligent ones, the sensitive ones, the ones they have been waiting for. Whatever butters your cabbage.

A Final Thought

So don't waste your whiteness.

If you were born into this world with this particular privilege, then it is your solemn obligation to be a good steward of that privilege. This, mind you, is privilege in *God's* world, not privilege in that pretendy world of the envious, where carping and clawing are the rule, and where every privilege is assumed to be obtained at the expense of somebody else.

If it is actual privilege, then a Christian has the responsibility to steward it with a grateful spirit of *noblesse oblige*. And of course *noblesse oblige* that is patronizing or supercilious isn't *noblesse oblige* at all. However, if it is the faux-sin of whiteness that the guilt-mongers are hurling at you, then you have the responsibility to just laugh at them and go on your way. And a black man with privileges that I don't have, but who has the same spirit of gratitude, should do exactly the same thing. We serve the same kind God, and we are not chafed by anything that God decided to give to somebody else.

If God has given you something, then you must not accuse Him of being a hard master, and then go off and bury it in a handkerchief (Luke 19:20–21). Although, actually, if we want to keep this parable current with the times, that worthless servant would have to go off to some designated safety zone at his college, wrap his whiteness in a handkerchief, give it to the trained counselor, and spend a soothing hour coloring pictures of the therapy puppies.

But the reason the master judges him out of his own mouth in this retold parable is because he didn't put his whiteness in the handkerchief at all. That entire hour was suffused in whiteness, from the ceiling to the floor, from the front door to the back door, and included the therapist, the coloring books, all the woke business, the hurt feelings, the appropriation of victimhood, the lot. He couldn't have spent a whiter hour than if he had gone off to the Benjamin Moore factory to dive head first into a vat of White Diamond OC-61.

CHAPTER SEVEN

Preeminently Stampedable

The inimitable Iowahawk recently tweeted this:

"Campuses today are a theatrical mashup of *1984* and *Lord of the Flies*, performed by people who don't understand these references."

To which we may also add the worthies who inhabit the indignation stampede grounds of Twitter, the people who are in charge of "best practices" protocols in use throughout all HR departments of America, and the shills of the new order who inhabit the editorial boards of our legacy media.

Now my purpose here is not really so much to critique the *content* of these contemporary moralistic stampedes, although their content is usually wicked and/or silly in equal measure, and thus quite deserving of anything we might throw at them. Rather my point lies elsewhere—although I do grant that I might get a jab or two in with regard to the content along the way.

But no, my larger purpose is simply to point out that they are in fact stampedes, that mankind in the first quarter of the 21st century remains a herd animal, and that the free thinking and liberated of today are wearing so many chains that they clank when they walk. They also wear blinders so that when they run into things there is even more clanking. Now it might seem strange to accuse individuals who are both bound *and* blind of being held captive by groupthink, but do not forget that all their peers are clanking also, which makes it really easy for today's nonconformists to locate and conform to one another just by sound alone.

Chains notwithstanding, the liberated mind of the contemporary scene is just a slow motion murmuration. Today's free thought is just an exercise in synchronized swimming, organized by some campus functionary in that great Olympic-sized pool that we built in Diversity Hall, located just behind the Center for the Elimination of Involuntary Wrongthink. Today's left embraces the free exchange of ideas the same way that the Spanish Inquisition protected academic freedom.

One Example, Fer Instance

Take, for example, the way we handle discussions of climate change. Take, for example, in the next section, how we are handling the issue of trans-sexuality.

It is not my purpose here to dismiss the idea of climate change as a scientific theorem, as fun as that might be. My point is simply to point out that it is enforced as though it were a dogma from Holy Mother Church sometime in 15th century Portugal. It brings to mind something H.L. Mencken said about democracy—a method for ascertaining truth by means of counting noses, and promulgating that truth afterwards with a club.

And the people perpetrating this farce will say, over and over again they will say, and with straight faces they will say, that this is a matter of scientific consensus. *Consensus?* Consensus is what scientific break-throughs *disturb*. Consensus is why Max Planck once said that science advances funeral by funeral. Thomas Kuhn showed us, or at least he showed some of us, that scientific advance is not a cumulative effort, like the formation of a coral reef. Scientific advance happens when certain brave individuals find themselves in the right position, a posi-tion that allows them to summon up the courage to merrily jettison— what's the plural for *consensus?* Science is surrounded with a debris field covered with notions that we used to think were true. And all those pieces are fragments of previous consensus.

Anybody who is enforcing the dictates of scientific consensus with a club, as in, threatening the jobs of dissenters, doesn't have the foggiest notion of what science ought to be. They do, however, know what a groupthink operation the 21st century is turning out to be. I know, let's call them climate deniers, thus to lump them in with Holocaust deniers.

Another Example, Fer Instance

Nor is it my purpose to point out that a man cannot become female by the simple expedient of declaring himself to be a female. Which, incidentally, he can't. No, my purpose here is to point out that just a few short years ago, virtually everybody agreed with that, agreeing with what is still my current position. So I missed a couple of mem-os. Sue me.

And now, just a few calendar years later, if you were, say, a hapless sportscaster who said on air that he didn't think it was right for Bruno to walk away with the women's cycling trophy (*again*), you would be frog-marched to the nearest window and promptly defenestrated.

No, it is worse than that. Suppose the sportscaster in question had read all the HR memos, and he *had* kept current, and let us say that he was a true conformist, with the backbone of a freshly baked maple bar right out of the oven, and consequently he had dutifully checked all the appropriate boxes, and then one fateful day a decision was announced that this coward was being promoted to the head position of something or other. All it would take for that promotion to fly away with the whistling wind would be for some enterprising soul to dig up some old tweets of his from ten years before, condemning the Bruno of that day. But he was tweeting the way he did back then precisely because he was such a conformist, doing what everybody else did. Guys, guys. It was *okay* back then.

That would not matter. Our sportscaster would be made to beg, and crawl, and grovel, and apologize, and to thank his persecutors for his upcoming and richly deserved defenestration, asking them to ensure, please, that he land on his head.

The Thing That Is Different Now

The great mass of mankind has always been a herd animal, and always will be. The great flock of sheep has always been a great flock of sheep. What is different about our era is not that we are sheep, but that we are delusional sheep. We have believed all the propaganda about how independent, and tough minded, and street savvy, and fiercely non-conformist we are.

Flocks of sheep have always trotted across the meadow together. It is just that today when they do it a bunch of them think they are "going Galt."

And another difference is that our contemporary shepherds are corrupt. There have always been shepherds (and sheep dogs) who understand the situation, and who are not affected by those things which spook the flock. But when the shepherds are wicked, they feed only themselves (Ezek. 34:2). Back in the day, the sheep knew who the shepherds were, knew who the sheep were, and also knew the difference between good and corrupt shepherds.

Today we act as much like sheep as ever we did, and all with a serene cluelessness about the true situation. The only way, really, for anyone to get free of this oppressive and claustrophobic situation is by embracing our true calling, which is to listen to the Good Shepherd. We need to hear His voice, and if we do hear His voice, He returns to us that which we surrendered, or thought we surrendered.

We give up to Him our grand pretense of individuality, which is the first step for Him in making us true individuals.

In the meantime, Mencken again: "The whole aim of practical politics is to keep the populace alarmed (and hence clamorous to be led to safety) by menacing it with an endless series of hobgoblins, all of them imaginary."[9]

9. *A Mencken Chrestomathy: His Own Selection of His Choicest Writing* (1949; New York: Vintage Books, 1982), 29.

CHAPTER EIGHT

The Devil's Smoothies

Well before the Revoice conference sought to carve out a place for smooth men in the evangelical and Reformed world, that way had already been prepared for them long before. Now it is true that John the Baptist was charged to make the rough places plain (Is. 40:4), so there is a sense in which such things are okay, but it took a rough man to do that. And therein lies a foundational point that must be learned and mastered.

Hard Teaching

As my father taught me many years ago, soft teaching is what creates hard hearts. Hard teaching is what creates soft hearts. The liberal mentality reverses this, and it is why, a short time after we have adopted their kindly suggestions, we see nothing but sad faces all around us.

The liberal mentality often appears years before the actual liberalism does, and the liberal mentality is what makes this kind of mistake so readily. Here are a few samples. If you spank your children, you are teaching them violence. If you practice Church discipline, you are chasing people away from the Church. If you preach the unvarnished Word of God, then people will grow hard in their love of a dogmatic blustering. In short, the liberal mentality believes that hard teaching creates hard hearts, and soft teaching is the kind of life coaching that creates soft hearts. This is a photo negative of the truth.

Whether or not Chick-fil-A has gone liberal in their recent rejection of the *be-less-chikken* stance, they most certainly are trying out the wisdom of the liberal mentality. Maybe if we give our enemies what they are demanding, this will turn them into our friends. The word we are looking for is appease, and it is vainly thought that appeasement is something other than surrender.

Gospel Should be Taken Like Whiskey, Straight

So a clear Word from God, authoritatively declared, is a hard word. Sin requires repentance and sin requires blood. It is a repentance we cannot muster, and it is the kind of pure blood that we do not have. We are therefore utterly lost.

And so it is that when the holy law of God is preached, and it falls on us like a collapsing mountain range, and when this is followed with a proclamation of free grace and forgiveness, a proclamation given to all those crushed beneath that mountain range of sheer holiness, a miracle of covenant kindness occurs. All our loathsome cadavers are dug out from the rubble, raised from the dead, and we are given the grace of walking in newness of life.

So in this sinful world, there is only one thing that can produce a tender heart. Allow me to say it again. In this sinful world, just one thing can bring about a tender heart. *And that one thing is the wrath of God.*

It is a wrath that was located in one place only, a wrath that descended in full fury from Heaven to Golgotha, that skull hill which held up the cross of Christ. The word propitiation sums up every aspect of this, and propitiation refers to how the death of Christ under the wrath of God was the genesis of any possible salvation. And this is how hard hearts are made tender.

It is the only way that hard hearts can be made tender. The quarry of God's wrath is the only place where these living stones can be quarried.

What About the Other Way?

And when you flip it around, you see another striking example of the same kind of reversal in expectations. Sinners with hard hearts love it when some soft preacher breaks out some feather duster of a sermon. With hearts like marble, with foreheads like flint, and with a brain full of snakes, the rebels want the preachers to be courteous enough to leave their sins alone. Many preachers are happy to oblige. Many preachers are trained to oblige. Many preachers cannot get ordained unless they promise to oblige.

But in contrast to the feather duster sermon, the faithful preacher brings a jackhammer, hooked up to a heavy duty air compressor. A jackhammer is what it takes to break up the hard hearts.

"Is not my word like as a fire? saith the LORD; and like a hammer that breaketh the rock in pieces?" (Jer. 23:29).

A Few Roughs With the Smooths

The Lord Himself pointed out that when everyone went out to see John the Baptist, they did not go out to see a smooth man (Matt. 11:8). That kind of man is found in kings' palaces. That kind of man wreaks his own peculiar kind of havoc out of an air-conditioned office, a place with plush carpeting, a polite receptionist, and a broad expanse of glass for a front wall, one that is cleaned twice a week.

The name of some great ecclesiastical Reformer, safely dead for centuries now, is etched in the glass as a way of honoring his memory, and were that Reformer to come back from the grave to see what is being done in his name, he would no doubt start the proceedings by throwing the coffee table of that swank reception area through the glass. The part of the glass where his name was.

Jesus taught us all about this particular juke move.

> Woe unto you, scribes and Pharisees, hypocrites! because ye build the tombs of the prophets, and garnish the sepulchres of the righteous, And say, If we had been in the days of our fathers, we would not have been partakers with them in the blood of the prophets. Wherefore ye be witnesses unto yourselves, that ye are the children of them which killed the prophets. Fill ye up then the measure of your fathers. (Matt. 23:29–32)

We do not meditate on this enough. Bragging on your forefathers in the faith is a good way to demonstrate a much greater likelihood that you would have been, had you been alive back then, part of the mob trying to get them run out of town. This is because soft boys are all about trying to fit in. And when angular prophets are alive and kicking, the way to fit in is to tsk under your breath about how off-putting Jeremiah has been lately. And then, centuries later, when

Jeremiah Hall is having the marble cornices installed, and the grand dedication is coming up, and you are organizing the press releases for the event, you have some trouble in your soul about whether that crack that Jesus made today in His teaching was really quite necessary. I mean, He didn't say that your job was not quite the ticket. He said it was a blood crime waiting to be filled to its full measure. He kind of thought it was a big deal.

> Now go, write it before them in a table, and note it in a book, that it may be for the time to come for ever and ever: That this is a rebellious people, lying children, children that will not hear the law of the LORD: Which say to the seers, See not; And to the prophets, Prophesy not unto us right things, speak unto us smooth things, prophesy deceits. (Is. 30:8–10)

We even have an industry dedicated to smooth things. We have conference circuits for seers who can't see. We have prophetic conferences which are overtly dedicated to saying the right thing while assiduously avoiding the actual saying of it, and the people are demanding even more of this theological bafflegab. Conference registrations are way up from last year! The demand for our smooth things is hot. We might even need some back-up fog machines this year.

Lies must be smooth. They all must be thrown into the devil's blender, and when you throw lies in the devil's blender, what you get are the devil's smoothies. Those things go down well too, cool to the throat, but it should be pointed out that they really unsettle the stomach. This is why the tables of Ephraim are covered with vomit and filthiness (Is. 28:8).

All Right Then

I have laid out my argument. I have quoted Jeremiah and Jesus and Isaiah. Why do you hesitate? Why do you still tolerate leaders who want to play footsie with world? All right then. You have forced me to it. I am going to quote C.S. Lewis. If there is one thing that move-with-the-times evangelicals have it is a deep appreciation for C.S. Lewis. If there is one thing that telling-the-world-it-is-quite-right Christians have it is a profound indebtedness to the Oxford don.

> In fact, we must at all costs not move with the times. We serve One who said 'Heaven and Earth shall move with the times, but my words shall not move with the times.'

> Jesus Christ did not say "Go into all the world and tell the world that it is quite right." The Gospel is something completely different. In fact, it is directly opposed to the world.[10]

---

10. *God in the Dock: Essays on Theology and Ethics*, ed. Walter Hooper (1970; Grand Rapids: William B. Eerdmans, 2014), 90, 293.

CHAPTER NINE

Idiocracy

Way back in the early eighties it was, and I read a book by Reagan's treasury secretary, a gent named William Simon. The book was called *Time for Truth*, and somewhere in the course of that book he explained (compellingly, in my view) why so many on what might be called the hard right have such a vulnerability to conspiratorial views. He said, Simon did, that this was the result of a charitable attribution of intelligence to their political foes.

Here is how the reasoning goes. Since it is plainly obvious that the progressive policies that are being foisted upon us are policies that amount to the ruination of the republic, and since it is assumed that the people doing the foisting are intelligent and well-educated and can therefore see what they are doing, it follows, as night follows day, that they are wrecking in the country on purpose. They must be in the pay of the commies. Since they are doing all of this on purpose, they must be doing it on purpose all together, and that is where you get the assumption that nefarious conspiracies are driving the whole thing.

Simon's *riposte* to this was telling. He simply gave his personal testimony. He said that he had been involved in decision-making at the highest levels of government for some time, and could testify that many of those who were making the destructo-decisions were absolutely clueless about the consequences and ramifications of what they were doing. No, it wasn't purposeful and malevolent destruction of all that ordinary people hold dear. Rather it was, in Sowell's great phrase, "self-congratulation as a basis for social policy."[11] Cluelessness firmly established on the foundational bedrock of invincible conceit.

The fact that such individuals are high-performance persons in many other areas of their lives matters not at all. They did not need to be idiots across the board, although idiocy does need to be given pride of place somewhere.

In fact, it is a peculiar form of idiocy to think that genuine expertise in one area of your life automatically transfers to any other—as though a man skilled in running a hedge fund, say, would thereby be automatically equipped to repair some circuits inside your malfunctioning smart phone, choosing for his only tools a pair of oven mitts and a couple popsicle sticks.

And this brings us to the somewhat dark assessment given by Ambrose Bierce.

> Idiot – A member of a large and powerful tribe whose influence in human affairs has always been dominant and controlling. The Idiot's activity is not confined to any special field of thought or action, but "pervades and regulates the whole."

11. *The Vision of the Anointed: Self-Congratulation as a Basis for Social Policy* (New York: BasicBooks, 1995).

He has the last word in everything; his decision is unappeal-
able. He sets the fashions and opinion of taste, dictates the
limitations of speech and circumscribes conduct with a dead-
line. (*The Devil's Dictionary*)

An Hypothesis

What we are dealing with, in many cases, is a peculiar configuration
of the *idiot savant*, one with the ratios reversed. The traditional *idiot
savant* is someone who excels in one area while being severely dis-
abled and helpless in most others. By way of contrast, our pestilent
ruling class is one which excels in many areas, is helpless in one, and
assumes to itself the absolute right to dictate to all the rest of us
from the crazed assumptions of that one area.

In other words, you have somebody who scored big time on his
SATs, got into Harvard, graduated into a six-figure job, is tech savvy,
married well, is a connoisseur of fine wines, and thinks that mini-
mum wage laws are a good idea that will actually help the poor.

And the conceit is incorrigible. The ignorance is adamantine. It
doesn't matter how many times the policy bursts into flames whenever it is applied. It doesn't matter how many thoughtful economists
show by rigorous argument that the policy is both wrong-footed and
wrong-headed. It doesn't matter that a casual ten-minute analysis can
reveal the fallacy. *It doesn't matter.*

But let me give three examples of things in this category that
should be obvious—because hope springs eternal.

I do not think that everything will become clear to everyone as
soon as folks read what I write. But there will come a time—because
thundering stupidity is never a sound long term policy—when the
frenzy is passed, when cooler heads have prevailed, and the insanities
of our generation have outlived their warranty. Future generations

will look back at what we were doing and ask themselves "what were they *thinking?*"

All we conservatives ask is a place in some future scholar's footnotes. "Not everyone went along with these notions . . ."

The Rich and the Poor

The received wisdom is that the rich are getting richer and the poor are getting poorer. You have heard a great deal about income inequality, and about what an awful business that is. Now my point here is not to focus on the ulcers of envy that make people say things like this. No, my point is the simple statistical blunder that is being made.

I will make some numbers up to illustrate the point. Suppose someone points out that forty years ago there were 10% of Americans living below the poverty line, and that 10% of Americans were upper middle class, and that the average income disparity between the two groups was 100K. And then today, a generation later, let us suppose that 12% of Americans were below the poverty line, 8% of Americans were upper middle class, and the average income disparity between them was 120K. Let us also suppose that these numbers are accurate, and not fudged in any way.

There is plenty here for a demagogue to work with. The Democratic nominee for president could fill stadiums up talking about this kind of stuff.

There are also cogent responses that I can't resist touching on before getting to the main point of silliness. Who calculates the poverty line? And in terms of actual purchasing power, are the people below the poverty line today better off than the people in the same status a generation ago? How many of the poor have smart phones compared to a generation ago? Is there a difference between *absolute* poverty and *relative* poverty? And so on we go, asking many salient questions.

But here is the central chicanery, the legerdemain, the conjuring trick. There is a difference between *statistical* categories and *actual people*. There is a stark difference between a *statistical* underclass and a *permanent* underclass. A generation ago, a bunch of the student couples below the poverty line—the Smiths, Murphys, Talcotts, and Peabodys—are now in the upper middle class. And some of the people in the upper middle class have drifted downward out of it.

In a society that contains as much upward mobility as ours does (which is to say, a great deal), to compare income disparity between statistical *groups* a generation ago and statistical *groups* now, as though we were talking about the same people, is the height of absurdity.

Did you know? Did you know that a generation ago there was a ten year differential between the graduating seniors and the second graders? And today, a full 40 years later, in a country that has put a man on the moon, did you know that *the second graders are no closer to graduation* than they were back then?

I would be willing to wipe away a tear for these abandoned second graders if that were warranted, but it isn't. They'll be fine.

Climate Change

We need a second example, so maybe we should talk about this strange weather god cult that all the authorities want us to join. They want us to dance around the great altar of the state, separating recyclables from regular trash, having our hotel towels not washed every day, and cutting ourselves with knives.

Ah, good old climate change.

When it comes to events that drive climate and weather, I wonder how much actual knowledge there is to be known. And I wonder also what percentage of that knowledge we currently have in our possession. In short, what does God know about all of this, and what fraction of this total amount of knowable knowledge do we know? Then you also have to throw into the mix the troublesome element of the things that we currently know that "just ain't so." That's an additional complication, right there.

Here are some relevant questions somebody should ask. Is the climate in fact actually changing? If it is changing, is this a bad thing for us, a good thing, or a net wash? If it is changing, and if it is a bad thing, are we in any way causing it? If we are causing it, is there any reasonable expectation that we might be able to reverse the effect we are having? And last, if there is a possibility of our action reversing this climate change, should the state have anything whatever to do with it?

Now of course there is obviously a possibility that the correct answer to every one of those questions is identical to what the most alarmed of all the alarmists might say. It is not as though anthropogenic climate change is a logical impossibility. However, comma.

A giant meteor headed straight toward St. Louis would be a great natural disaster, but it would be a-simple-to-understand disaster. A big rock is going to create a crater in the heartland the size of Rhode Island. And it would be a threat with one variable. All the amateur astronomers could be invited to look at it coming, and to do the math themselves. *Hmmm*, we would say to ourselves. We had better mobilize.

But a weather system has millions of variables, not one, and climate might be understood as a "weather system" of weather systems. How many variables are we talking about? How many inputs into the system? How complicated is the question? Do we even know what we are talking about?

Consider my earlier questions and apply them to the Medieval Warming Period. Was the climate in fact actually changing? *Yes, it did, undeniably.* If it did change, was this a bad thing for us, a good thing, or a net wash? *From all the reports, it was a good thing. Greenland was actually a fun place.* If it changed, was this caused in any way by the activities of men? *This was long before the industrial revolution and so it is hard to imagine how we might have contributed.* If man caused it, was there any reasonable expectation that they might have been able to reverse the effect they had? *No.* And last, if there was a possibility of our action reversing this climate change, should the state have had anything whatever to do with it? *No. If we had given plenipotentiary powers to Sven the Marauder, so that he might give himself fully to the task of fighting climate change, caused by bad Vikings who had their hotel towels washed every day, the chance are pretty good that he would have used those powers, not to crack down on the hotel towel travesty, but rather to do some more marauding.*

Chicken Little alarmists have been predicting the end for quite some time now. "If we don't take immediate action, within five years it will be too late." Well, then, since we have apparently missed all the deadlines, established for us by Men of Science, then there is clearly nothing for it but to shrug our shoulders, and enjoy whatever time it is we have left.

"Tell us what is to come hereafter, that we may know that you are gods; do good, or do harm, that we may be dismayed and terrified" (Is. 41:23, ESV).

Some weather god.

The Transsexual Phantasmagorithon

I saved the fruitiest one for last. The final and utter frozen limit is the mass hallucination that has taken a firm hold throughout our intelligentsia. Remember that these are people who, in most areas of life, do well for themselves. They know when to buy and sell their stocks. They have drivers' licenses. They do not shovel their walks in summer, and they do not mow their lawns in winter. So everything seems fine.

And yet somehow . . .

They have bought into the supposition—hook, line, sinker, and the fisherman's waders—that someone can simply decide that they are not actually the sex that God assigned to them. In addition, they have marshaled the full force of the law in order to demand that this authoritative decision must be respected by all and sundry, in the teeth of the evidence. Further, it has been determined by the enlightened one that those who refuse to go along with this naked-emperor-charade will be deemed to be the "anti-science" faction.

A dude can have trillions of cells with XY chromosomes in his body, with each one of those cells testifying to the fact that this is in fact a dude, and yet, if he applies some bright red XX lipstick to his XY lips, this somehow changes everything.

As the old Southern proverb has it, some folks' corn bread ain't quite done in the middle.

There is a common saying or riddle that comes in many forms, but the essence of it is this. How many legs does a dog have if we call the tail a leg? The answer is four, because calling the tail a leg doesn't make it one.

We are just about at peak frenzy with this one, but the nature of the frenzy is different depending on whether we are talking about the secular world or the Christian world. The secular world is in the grip of a delusion; confusion has them by the throat. This is not the case in the Christian world. We are not confused the way they are. We know that the girls are girls and the guys are guys. Not confused on the issue at all. We are just cowards. Cowardice has us by the throat.

CHAPTER TEN

Heading Off a Woke Thanksgiving

So Thanksgiving is tomorrow, and perhaps you will be seated next to a garrulous and somewhat combative uncle, a man who drinks in his opinions at MoveOn.org, and who has voted for Bernie more than once. He lives in Massachusetts and really likes the way things are going out there. Thanksgivings in Arkansas are rough on him, and so he starts up various wrangles with his troglodyte relatives simply as a way of coming up for air. We should have more sympathy for him than we do.

Rewinding History

We live in a time when people are trying to rewind all kinds of history. Columbus Day is now Indigenous Peoples Day in many places, and this obviously has ramifications for the mythic account of our Thanksgiving holiday. That origin actually happened though, as

Lewis taught us, that "mythic" need not be false. The Pilgrims held a three day feast after they brought in their first harvest in 1621, and it was attended by almost one hundred members of the Wampanoag tribe and about half that number of Englishmen.

But it is also a mythic origin story because it didn't start to turn into what we know as our Thanksgiving until over two centuries later when Abraham Lincoln made his declaration, and subsequently a lot of meaning was retroactively projected back onto the first Thanksgiving. And even the official declaration in 1863 cannot be considered as a voice of unanimity because Lincoln was expressing gratitude for the Union victory at Gettysburg a few months before, and there was still two more years of fratricidal conflict to come. We were spang in the middle of a war over the meaning of these United States.

It slowly evolved until it reached its apotheosis in Norman Rockwell's version of the Thanksgiving dinner. And since that time our self-anointed debunkers and deconstructionists have been busy drawing mustaches on everyone in that painting, starting with the ladies. There was more to *that* move than we supposed at the time, and we should freely confess that we should have been more alert.

Nevertheless, the tumultuous history of Thanksgiving has left the door open for many postmodern wielders of corrosive acids to step in with their view that Thanksgiving really ought to be renamed something like Genocide Awareness Day. But as is the fashion of debunkers, our modern naysayers often cannot be troubled with un-derstanding what actually happened throughout our actual history, and so they resort to the simple expedient of putting a different film into the retrospective projector.

So frankly, I do not recommend all-out combat with your uncle, for that would distress your grandmother. But perhaps, as you listen to him vent, you can interject some sensible observations at strategic places, and demur just a little bit. But mind your manners and don't throw any stuffing.

Narratives, New and Old

Here's the new narrative. White people landed in New England, and after one year held a feast at which Native Americans were in attendance, and the white people eerily set the stage for all the infamy to follow, and they did this by hogging the mashed potatoes.

Now the way for you to avoid a woke Thanksgiving is by paying close attention to the names of the two groups in my second paragraph at the beginning—Wampanoag and Englishmen—and the names of the two groups in the paragraph just before this one—white people and Native Americans. There is *way* more to this than you might suppose.

It is the difference between history as photographed by Ansel Adams and history as painted by a purblind impressionist. I am talking about the importance of detail.

Tribes, Not Vibes

So let us begin with this part of it with a plain assertion. Anybody who talks about the settling of North America as though it were a cohesive group called "white people" doing the settling and a group of indigenous flower children being displaced by the disembarking whites is someone who probably ought to stay out of the conversation. Except for your uncle, who started it.

The inhabitants of North America when Columbus landed were divided into many tribes, multiple tribes, and these tribes had different languages, customs, histories, and characteristics. Quite a number of these tribes were mortal enemies, one to another. And to make the whole situation even more festive, the newcomers were also divided into different tribes, and *they* had different languages, customs, histories, and characteristics. A number of these tribes were mortal enemies, one to another.

White tribes would war with each other, like the French and English did. Red tribes would war with each other, like the Comanche and Apache. Red tribes would go to war with white tribes, like the Wampanoag in King Philip's War, with the Mohawk fighting on the side of the English. And white tribes would grievously mistreat oppress red tribes, as happened to the Five Civilized Tribes (Choctaw, Chickasaw, Seminole, Creek, and Cherokee), culminating in the Trail of Tears. And I use white and red above, not as *my* categories, but rather as a way of illustrating that when you zoom out that far, such that those are the two identifying characteristics that you see, then by that point you understand *almost nothing.*

Correction. You do understand one thing, and that is the line of propaganda you are being fed.

The phenomenon of Caucasoid peoples running around is certainly an item of interest to biologists, but has nothing relevant whatever to do with political history, military history, or the history of immigration, expansion, or trade. There is not, and never has been, a Parliament of White People. There is no covenant binding white people together, and they have never made any collective decision whatever. This means that if guilt can be assigned to malevolent decisions only, and white people considered as such have never made *any* decisions, then we need to be done talking about what whites did to reds. Whites have done nothing to reds for the simple reason that whites have never done anything.

There *is* such a thing as collective responsibility or guilt, but this only takes shape as tribes, nations, or states make their decisions and act accordingly. And red-heads have never made one decision together, in the history of the world, and I think we should stop blaming them for it.

Of course, there is a superficial appearance to the contrary that can be misleading to some. For example, when General Sherman attacked the peace-loving Sioux and burned their great city Atlan-ta to the ground . . . excuse me? I am informed by my researchers that Atlan-ta was a Celtic settlement, inhabited largely by a white tribe called the Jorjawns. *Blog and Mablog* regrets the error.

So the Comanche were not Quakers, and were about as blood-thirsty and appalling as one might be able to imagine. And all things considered, the Cherokee were a decent folk, and made a good faith effort to assimilate to the new situation. The Cherokee got ripped off. And further south, the Aztecs deserved everything they got, good and hard. I have shed about as many tears for the Aztecs as I have for the Amorites—which is to say, not very many.

Power and Envy

Armed with the basic facts, you will be enabled to avoid getting woke in between the turkey and the pie.

But there is one more weapon you will need in your arsenal. You will need to understand what is going on *now*, and not just what happened back in the day, over the last four centuries or so. Not only so, but you will need to understand *why* it is going on.

Critical Race Theory reduces everything to power differentials, and then looks at those differentials through the grimy lens of envy. According to these folks, everything back then was a power play, and the people running the power play, by definition, were the ones who wound up with the power. And since America in its thriving mid-twentieth century heyday was populated at the top with white-skinned people with Anglo Saxon names, then they must have been the ones running the power play.

The fact that the victors may well have been greedy does not prevent those who lost to them from being envious. And because envy is a wasting disease, a wasting disease that seeks to deck itself out in the language of virtue, it blurs all historical distinction, and talks a great deal about social justice. We, on the other hand, like to talk about a little thing we call justice justice.

So I am far more interested in recognizing who is hungry for power now. Who is running the current power plays? Who wants to take all our money in order to appease their capricious weather god? Who wants to regulate the education of my grandchildren? Who wants to dictate to me what pronouns I may and may not use? Who wants the federal government to grow up into swollen shapes that border on the macabre?

Right. Everybody who is currently running for the Democratic nomination for president. And you are talking to someone who voted for *Bernie* more than once.

CHAPTER ELEVEN

Rez Zoh Looo Tion #9

I took my troubles down to Madame Ruth
You know that gypsy with the gold-capped tooth
She's got a pad down on Thirty-Fourth and Vine
Selling little bottles of REZ ZO LOOO TION number nine.

Now I know that there are some dissimilarities between Resolution #9, passed this last year by the Southern Baptist Convention, and Love Potion #9, as trenchantly described for us in that instructive song by the Clovers.[12] But at the same time, I do fear that the same basic outcome is going to come to pass either way, which is to say that our protagonist is going to wind up "kissing everything in sight." Including commies.

12. "On Critical Race Theory And Intersectionality," Southern Baptist Convention, Birmingham, Alabama, 2019, sbc.net/resolutions/2308/resolution-9--on-critical-race-theory-and-intersectionality.

In preparation for that sad day, I thought it would be good if I provided some commentary on the resolution itself. So here goes.

Color Commentary

> WHEREAS, Concerns have been raised by some evangelicals over the use of frameworks such as critical race theory and intersectionality; and

"Concerns have been raised" is kind of understating it. The Southern Baptist Convention is in an uproar over it is more like it. This is like saying that General Beauregard made a point to raise some concerns that he had at Fort Sumter, and that Major Anderson, commanding the Union forces, replied with some concerns of his own.

> WHEREAS, Critical race theory is a set of analytical tools that explain how race has and continues to function in society, and intersectionality is the study of how different personal characteristics overlap and inform one's experience; and

Just a set of analytical tools here. Kind of like an epistemic screwdriver. It is just lying in the tool box there, exuding neutrality. Critical race theory simply "explains" how race has in the past functioned in society, and how it continues to function in society. It does this in ways that are compelling, self-evident and undeniable, sort of like the formula for force, mass and acceleration: Force (N) = mass (kg) $\times$ acceleration (m/s2). The only people who deny this kind of self-evident whiteness-is-bad thing are science-deniers, and people who don't want to lose their reputations and jobs.

WHEREAS, Critical race theory and intersectionality have been appropriated by individuals with worldviews that are contrary to the Christian faith, resulting in ideologies and methods that contradict Scripture; and

Unfortunately, this thinking goes, the bad guys snuck in, and crept up behind this set of innocent analytic tools, and then stole them, taking them off to use for their own nefarious purposes. In this view, CRT is like the forbidden but good fruit in the garden of Eden, with the serpent enticing them to stray.

But rather CRT was invented by the bad guys, concocted by them, devised by them, engineered by them, and I could keep coming up with different synonymous verbs, but I trust you get the point. The reason this stew tastes the way it does is because it came right out of the devil's pot.

WHEREAS, Evangelical scholars who affirm the authority and sufficiency of Scripture have employed selective insights from critical race theory and intersectionality to understand multifaceted social dynamics; and

Ah, you know how tricky those multifaceted social dynamics are. Selective insights? What is the principle of selection? I believe the question has been raised before, but it is pretty evident that it needs to be raised again—by what standard?

WHEREAS, The Baptist Faith and Message states, "[A]ll Scripture is totally true and trustworthy. It reveals the principles by which God judges us, and therefore is, and will remain to the end of the world, the true center of Christian

> union, and the supreme standard by which all human con-
> duct, creeds, and religious opinions should be tried" (Article
> I); and

Amen. That's a good one. What's it doing in here?

> WHEREAS, General revelation accounts for truthful in-
> sights found in human ideas that do not explicitly emerge
> from Scripture and reflects what some may term "common
> grace"; and

Common grace is found in all sorts of places, and we need not have a proof text before we can accept what God has given us through common grace. Through common grace, we understand that objects fall when dropped at 9.8 meters per second squared, that water flows downhill, and that whiteness is a great evil that has blackened the sky and smokes to the sun. We all understand these things by common grace. Except for white people. They don't get it at all.

> WHEREAS, Critical race theory and intersectionality alone
> are insufficient to diagnose and redress the root causes of
> the social ills that they identify, which result from sin, yet
> these analytical tools can aid in evaluating a variety of human
> experiences; and

What analytic tool shall we use to examine our choices of analytic tools? If CRT and intersectionality are tools that are being offered to us, how shall we determine if they are good tools or lousy ones?

WHEREAS, Scripture contains categories and principles
by which to deal with racism, poverty, sexism, injustice, and
abuse that are not rooted in secular ideologies; and

Yes, it does. So why are we fooling around with CRT and intersectionality again?

It is one thing to pillage the Egyptians for their gold, and quite another to go dumpster diving in Egypt and to come back with a broken
DVD player, an opened package of hot dog buns, and a used grapefruit
rind, and then tell the rest of us that common grace is a Kuyperian necessity. Yes, it is, but I still don't want your grapefruit rind.

WHEREAS, Humanity is primarily identified in Scripture as
image bearers of God, even as biblical authors address various audiences according to characteristics such as male and
female, Jew and Gentile, slave and free; and

Yes, humanity is identified as being God's image bearers, and so it
is truly distressing when they go off and do stuff like this.

WHEREAS, The New Covenant further unites image bearers by creating a new humanity that will one day inhabit the
new creation, and that the people of this new humanity,
though descended from every nation, tribe, tongue, and people, are all one through the gospel of Jesus Christ (Eph. 2:16;
Rev. 21:1–4, 9–14); and

This is the second time I have had to say *amen*. I am starting to get
nervous. I will try to watch it in the future.

WHEREAS, Christian citizenship is not based on our differences but instead on our common salvation in Christ—the source of our truest and ultimate identity; and

Darn it. Amen again.

WHEREAS, The Southern Baptist Convention is committed to racial reconciliation built upon biblical presuppositions and is committed to seeking biblical justice through biblical means; now, therefore, be it

This is what I would call a real losing streak. Can't object to this either.

RESOLVED, That the messengers to the Southern Baptist Convention meeting in Birmingham, Alabama, June 11–12, 2019, affirm Scripture as the first, last, and sufficient authority with regard to how the Church seeks to redress social ills, and we reject any conduct, creeds, and religious opinions which contradict Scripture; and be it further

Okay, I get it. They are trying to lull me to sleep. They want me to drop my guard. But I will stay on guard because I can hear a couple of porch climbers now, trying to jimmy open the window of our Pauline liberties.

RESOLVED, That critical race theory and intersectionality should *only* be employed as analytical tools subordinate to Scripture—not as transcendent ideological frameworks; and be it further

Okay, here we go. We have found the poison in the pot, the snake in the grass, the toad in the punch bowl, the cockroach on the spaghetti, the slug in the salad, the . . . um, the difficulty.

Do you realize how many excuses this provides for how many poisonous ideologies? Dialectical materialism should only be employed as an analytical tool subordinate to Scripture, and not as a transcendental ideological framework. So long as the insights of white supremacists (note: actual ones) are not treated as an absolute, and we apply their views selectively, keeping them subordinate to Scripture at all times . . .

Sometimes Nancy has to stop me from going into the kitchen to grab some tea cups so that I can start throwing them against the wall.

Not really.

> RESOLVED, That the gospel of Jesus Christ alone grants
> the power to change people and society because "he who
> started a good work in you will carry it on to completion until
> the day of Christ Jesus" (Phil. 1:6); and be it further

After CRT has neutrally analyzed you and discovered that your central difficulty is your whiteness, then we are willing to say that Jesus Christ alone can forgive you of that great sin of whiteness.

But I don't need Jesus to forgive me for the things *He* did. I need Him to forgive me for the things that *I* did.

> RESOLVED, That Southern Baptists will carefully analyze
> how the information gleaned from these tools are employed
> to address social dynamics; and be it further

Southern Baptists will carefully analyze how this is being used, eh? As a sage once put it, somebody is always up to something, and the rest of them are up to something else. If the past is prologue, let me explain to you *how* they will analyze it. What are the central ingredients to such analysis? Well, you will need a committee, and you will need a back room, and you will need the committee to pop the results of their review on the convention with about thirty-five minutes available for debate. The review of this careful analysis will be prefaced with "open wide, boys."

> RESOLVED, That Southern Baptist churches and institu-
> tions repudiate the misuse of insights gained from critical
> race theory, intersectionality, and any unbiblical ideologies
> that can emerge from their use when absolutized as a world-
> view; and be it further

Like what? Name one. Be specific. Don't condemn a generic "misuse of insights." We stand firmly against anything icky that may have come from all of this, but we will be most coy when asked to define "icky." Now if they had said something like "unbiblical ideologies, such as the published frothings of Dr. James H. Cone . . ." that would be something we could all work with.

But as it appears to be going . . . and Nathan saith unto David, Behold, thou are the man. And David replied that he knew and understood that we live in a broken world, and that he was coming to understand just how much that brokenness had affected him personally, and that he was preparing his heart to take full and complete ownership of that brokenness. He was also prepared to say that it was most likely that mistakes had in fact been made, and that an investigation would be opened at the earliest opportunity to find out who had been principally responsible.

> RESOLVED, That we deny any philosophy or theology that fundamentally defines individuals using categories identified as sinful in Scripture rather than the transcendent reality shared by every image bearer and divinely affirmed distinctions; and be it further

I am frankly astonished that Tom Ascol managed to slip a condemnation of Revoice into this thing. He is *way* tricksier than I thought.

Although I am somewhat puzzled by the definition of "fundamentally defines" as opposed to "defines." We need to have one of the Guardian Committees sort that out. They can tell us it is all okay when there are five minutes left.

> RESOLVED, That while we denounce the misuse of critical race theory and intersectionality, we do not deny that ethnic, gender, and cultural distinctions exist and are a gift from God that will give Him absolute glory when all humanity gathers around His throne in worship because of the redemption accomplished by our resurrected Lord; and be it finally

Except for the whiteness. There will be no whiteness gathered around the throne. Right? Or did I misunderstand something?

> RESOLVED, That Southern Baptist churches seek to exhibit this eschatological promise in our churches in the present by focusing on unity in Christ amid image bearers and rightly

celebrate our differences as determined by God in the new creation.

And the way we will celebrate our differences is by following the higher path that critical race theory has taught us. For a hypothetical example, say that a Southern Baptist church has a candidate for pastor who is black, not that there is anything wrong with *that*, and who is also something of a lefty, and of course there is everything wrong with that, and let us say that he falls just shy of the vote margin needed to call him as a pastor. What we have learned from CRT (since everything is a matter of power) is that the white members who voted against him must have been drawing on their whiteness, and not on the priesthood of all believers. This is a wicked, wicked crime, and so those guilty of voting *no* need to be accused of racism and placed under Church discipline. This is all okay, because critical race theory is a set of neutral analytic tools.

Conclusion

And so anyone who actually believes that CRT is a useful and neutral analytic tool—and this currently includes the entire SBC, as they stated it out loud in solemn assembly, without turning vermilion red, I am afraid—is being a chump of the highest order and rank. If chumps had a navy, we are talking about flag rank, we are talking about a bevy of admirals. And if the top admirals don't do something about this travesty quick, we are going to see the whole fleet on the beach.

CHAPTER TWELVE

Rabshakeh, Chief of the Pronoun Police

So imagine for yourself the sweetest little boy in the church, one whose mind turns naturally to edifying themes—the kind of meditative theme inspired by reflections on a porcelain figurine of the infant Samuel at prayer. Suppose further that this boy has plump cheeks, with kind of a rosy tint or glow, and those cheeks have been routinely pinched by all the pious church ladies, and they have been telling him for ever so many years that a face so cherubic should really be blessing the professors at some select seminary.

By now many of you have heard that J.D. Greer, president of the Southern Baptist Convention, caused something of a stir a few days ago when in a podcast he urged Christians to lean toward "pronoun hospitality" in their dealings with those in the trans world who have been taught to demand that the whole world cater to their sensibilities.

Since that stir happened, there have been a few more developments on that front, and J.D. Greear has now endorsed the approach of Andrew Walker, an approach which was considerably more conservative than what Greer had initially sounded like.[13]

So I understand that this particular controversy is largely over. And yet I have a few things I would like to add. What to do? Now I understand that this is as though there was a bar fight in your town, the police broke it up, and then you went down there a few hours later to throw some chairs.

But still. Whether this particular controversy is over, the whole situation that gave rise to it is by no means over—and Christians really need to get our thinking straight on this issue. And in order to do that we have to distinguish where we actually are from where a large number of people want to pretend we actually are.

A Matter of Evangelism

Whenever we interact with the world of unbelievers, we should always have evangelism on our heart and mind. But there are two very different contexts for evangelism, and those two contexts are called war and peace respectively.

Having a heart for evangelism must never be confused with the condition of not being able to tell the difference between war and peace.

Let us imagine a man who is a Christian and a cop. He is part of the riot control squad, and let us suppose further that he has in the past fulfilled his role in that job when some sexual deviance protest got out of hand. Now imagine this same man as living next door to a transsexual, one who has on occasion borrowed his lawn mower,

---

13. Rod Dreher, "J.D. Greear Clarifies Pronoun Stance," *The American Conservative*, November 27, 2019, https://www.theamericanconservative.com/dreher/jd-greear-clarifies-pronoun-stance-lgbt/

and who is open to hearing the gospel. They have had some good talks, with a spirit of grace pervading. Should this cop's prayers, and thoughts, and hopes, and concerns be for evangelism *in both instances*? Yes, certainly, of course. But his presentation is different, and is different by necessity.

Those who cannot make this very simple distinction are pacifists in principle, whether or not they think of themselves that way. They assume that if a Christian is ever in a situation where he opts for confrontation, then this must be because that Christian has abandoned all concern for evangelism. They assume that he must not love his enemies because he has some.

The problem with this assumption is that this is not what Jesus did, it is not found anywhere in Scripture, it is not the approach of the historic Church, and it maketh no sense, man.

So Make a Basic Distinction

The world really is full of busted up people, and evangelical Christians have always been in the forefront of ministering to such people. We do not need to prove to anyone that our heart leans toward that type of kindness. In reply to the secularist charge that we are hardhearted, I would point out (mildly) that we have founded countless hospitals, orphanages, homeless shelters, crisis pregnancy centers, urban missions, and we have done it by donating our own money and time. When you compare this to the secularist kind of generosity which funds *its* maladroit efforts to help the less fortunate by sending men with guns to collect back taxes from small business owners who are struggling to make it, you will perhaps pardon me if the odor of their self-congratulation does not smell as sweet to me as they think it ought to.

Evangelical believers have been working with the downtrodden for centuries. But as our discussion of this goes forward, please allow us to maintain a basic distinction that our faith teaches us, which is the distinction between *helping* the wrecked and *applauding* the wreckage.

Even when it comes to mercy ministry of the most basic kind—soup kitchens, rehab, homeless shelters—what would an experienced ministry think of a demand that we should start ministering to drunks by signing on to an Alcoholic Empowerment Campaign that insisted that the bums being helped had to be referred to as members of the Alternative Sobrieties community. "This may not be *your* sobriety, but it is the sobriety that they have chosen."

The Pronoun Police

And this is what gets us to the point of the sexual madhouse we are currently trying to live in. The use of pronouns today is a deadly serious thing. It is not a matter of manners, or avoiding a *faux pas*. It is not a matter of showing courtesy to non-Christians. This is not about courtesy; rather, it is about coercion. It is not social graces; it is social engineering. We are having to stave off orc-talk.

So we are dealing with the Pronoun Police—and they are entirely willing to wreck your life and your livelihood over this issue. So this is not a matter of showing hospitality. That's not the question. It is not a matter of showing grace. That is not it either. It is not a question of showing courtesy, or kindness. No. *It is a question of courage.*

I have hit this point a number of times over the years, and the truth of it—always self-evident—has only grown more self-evident as the years have gone by.

The Christian faith is under siege. Our dear city is surrounded, and Rabshakeh is riding around below the walls, taunting us.

In a time like this, when a high premium should be placed on *courage*, the pressure is on all our poohbahs and solons to figure out a path to *compromise*, and all while maintaining that it is a question of deep *conviction*. Hospitality is a good thing, right?

It is as though our riot control cop ran away because he got scared, and then tried to represent it as a concern for preserving a sharing and teachable moment with his neighbor.

CHAPTER THIRTEEN

Exceptions and Loopholes

The downward spiral we are now riding when it comes to sexual ethics did not begin with *Obergefell*. It did not begin in the homosexual enclaves and bath houses. Homosexuals did not want to participate in the great marriage joke until after heterosexuals had turned it into the great marriage joke. But once the center had given way, and the widening gyre began, and easy divorce was first tolerated, then accepted, and then in some quarters celebrated, all the rest of this sexual clown car parade was inevitable.

And the pressures and realities connected to all of this are by no means absent in the conservative sectors of the Church. For example, Wayne Grudem recently stated that he had reworked his views on whether abuse was grounds for divorce, and he had gone back to the text in response to a few horrendous situations he had encountered. Now this is an entirely appropriate thing to do, and I am not here disputing his textual work, one way or the other.

What I am doing is pointing out that when there have been two scripturally legitimate grounds for divorce that have been slowly expanded into loopholes, then what makes us think this process will stop if we find that there are three scripturally legitimate grounds for divorce? If there is legitimacy here at all, then there is a border between legitimacy and illegitimacy, and that border will have to be articulated and defended by pastors and counselors with backbone.

What I Am Not Talking About

When it comes to the question of the permanence of marriage, I hold to what I believe to be the standard Reformed position. Even though this is the last day of November, this is less a qualification than it is a circumscription—I am not attempting to prove anything one way or the other about this position. I am simply noting it as the place I am reasoning from.

And to be specific, I believe that marriage is created by God, not man, and that what God has joined together, let no man put asunder. Marriages are not simply contracts which can be voided when the parties to the contract feel like it. Marriage is a covenant, and God is one of the parties to the covenant. This means that a marriage cannot be dissolved except under the two basic conditions that are set forth in Scripture. Those two conditions I believe to be the infidelity of adultery, and willful desertion. When one of those two conditions pertain, I believe the party sinned against may obtain a lawful divorce, and in principle, is free to remarry.

And What I *Am* Talking About

A great deal depends on whether these two exceptions are treated as exceptions, or whether they get treated as increasingly elastic loopholes.

And so what do I mean by exceptions becoming loopholes? I mean that all adultery is infidelity, but not all infidelity, particularly in seed form, is the kind of adultery that grants the liberty of a divorce. If a husband ogles a magazine cover in the checkout line at the supermarket, then that is infidelity and Jesus warns us about it. But it is not the kind of adultery that triggers an acceptable divorce.

If abuse is shown to be a separate third category that allows for divorce, or if it is included under one of the existing two categories (as being tantamount to willful desertion), the opportunity is immediately created to do the same thing. And that is to say that abuse is grounds for divorce, and then proceed to significantly expand the definition of abuse. True abuse is something that cops can tell you about, as well as pastors. Say a man beats his wife up several times a week—that is abuse, and that would be what Grudem is talking about. But suppose the definition of abuse is expanded to include those instances when a husband wasn't "there for her, when she needed him most." What if it now includes a husband who won't agree to something his wife really wants to do? And suppose that he puts his foot down in a rhetorical manner that indicated he wanted to be crowned as king of the meatheads?

A Quick Review

Here is a statement of the two exceptions as articulated by theologians who were *not* participating in what might be called our modern "exception inflation."

Although the corruption of man be such as is apt to study arguments, unduly to put asunder those whom God hath joined together in marriage; yet nothing but adultery, or such wilful desertion as can no way be remedied by the Church or civil magistrate, is cause sufficient of dissolving the bond of marriage; wherein a public and orderly course of proceeding is to be observed; and the persons concerned in it, not left to their own wills and discretion in their own case. (WCF 24.6)

There are three significant points to be made from this, and they each indicate that the Westminster Assembly contained a number of experienced pastors.

First, they noted that when it came to how people want to get out of unhappy marriages, they are apt to "study arguments." They are people with an acceptable conclusion who are on the hunt for usable premises. This tendency is assigned to the corruption of man. We must be careful of this *because we live in a corrupt time*.

Second, the two exceptions are stated. They say that there are no grounds for divorce except for these two situations. "Yet nothing but." Adultery is the first situation, and that would be defined as sexual intercourse contrary to the standard of fidelity set down in Scripture. And note that the second condition is not simply "willful desertion." It is "willful desertion" that can in "no way be remedied by the Church or by the civil magistrate." In other words, there might be a desertion, but we still need to see if the pastor and elders, or perhaps the sheriff, can fetch the straying spouse back.

The third pastoral note is that these determinations should be made by third parties, and not by the disputants themselves.

The Case of Separation

Now what happens when you have a situation that is obviously intolerable, but the two exceptions above do not seem to pertain? It is intolerable because the cops are getting called every third night or so, but there is no sexual infidelity, and the husband, who is the aforementioned king of the meatheads, says that he is not deserting his wife, but really wants to remain married to her. What then?

I think a biblical case for separation (*not* divorce) can be made, and the basis for it is here:

> And unto the married I command, yet not I, but the Lord, Let
> not the wife depart from her husband: But and if she depart,
> let her remain unmarried, or be reconciled to her husband: and
> let not the husband put away his wife. (1 Cor. 7:10–11)

This is talking about a situation where the wife who departs from her husband does not have a biblical basis for a divorce (which would give her the right to remarry). Paul expressly excludes that option. And so Paul says that she should stay right where she is. He is saying this in the light of his cryptic "not I, but the Lord" phrasing.

I do not take this as Paul outlining the inspired parts of 1 Corinthians 7, contrasting them with the mere Pauline opinion parts. Rather, I believe that Paul is referring to the Lord's teaching on marriage in the course of His earthly ministry, where He was teaching in the context of Israel, where both husband and wife were members of the covenant. In that setting, the Lord gave us one legitimate basis for divorce, which was adultery. Paul is referring to that first exception here, and it is the basis for him saying that the wife must remain single if she leaves. If she does not remain unmarried, she becomes an adulteress—committing adultery against the king of the meatheads.

Elsewhere in this chapter, Paul says "I, not the Lord" and he is *there* talking about a new situation that had arisen. This is apostolic instruction, not dominical instruction. The gospel had by this point gone out into the Gentile world, and the new and relatively common situation of mixed marriages was presenting pastoral questions. One of the partners had been converted, and the other one had not been converted. So the Corinthians wrote Paul and asked if it was okay to be married to a pagan. Yes, Paul says. To have sex with him? Yes, Paul says. But what if there are kids? Won't they be contaminated (1 Cor. 7:14)? No, Paul says. They will be holy.

Now in *this* setting, Paul is saying that he recommends against separating, but if she separates against this advice, what does he require? He requires that the woman who depart remain unmarried, or else to be reconciled to her husband. It is clear that he requires this because if she takes up with another man, she will be committing adultery. That means the first century Church had the option of a married couple living apart, but where there were still marital obligations in place. In other words, what we would call a separation.

And here is where things can go off the rails. This is where exceptions can become loopholes.

In our pastoral ministry, there have been situations where it really was necessary for the wife to "move out of range." And our church has consistently sought to provide wives with the kind of protection that a church can give in that kind of situation. Men are sinners.

The Hard Part

But, as *should* always be remembered, women are sinners also. A wife who is abused by her husband should obviously be protected by her church. But a wife who falsely accuses her husband of abuse should be disciplined by her church. *Believe all women* is the devil's lie. This is just another way of saying that husbands, as members of the congregation, require the protection of the church as well. This protection must include things like due process, two or three witnesses, and judges who don't come to the weighing of the evidence with minds already made up.

There, I said it. Under the cover of a waning No Quarter November, I come out squarely in favor of justice and equity. Make of it what you will.

Viewing the NQN 2019 Game Film

Well then, we have completed our second edition of No Quarter November, and with none of the support staff being hurt or maimed in any way. And as you may recall, last year I followed up all the NQN doings with a *post mortem*. The salient questions were, at that time, how did the month go, and why did we do it?

Providing you with that explanation last year seemed like a good idea back then, and because it *still* seems like a good idea, I would like to report on NQN 2019 as well. How did it go this year? And what exactly are we trying to accomplish? These remain reasonable questions, no?

First, the Stats

I wanted to go over some of the stats with you. I do this mindful of the solemn warning given by Gregory of Nazianzus when he cautioned us about tooting our own kazoo. So we want to be careful not to have this be a braggy-brag thing, but rather something more akin to a report issued to the joint-stockholders. I mean, you guys put up with a lot of grief for liking what we are trying to accomplish out here, and so sometimes it must feel like you are the lone weirdo in your church, denomination, or even at the meetings of the Chimacum County Clogging Association. Be encouraged. There are many others out there, other lone weirdos.

So we gave you a report last year, and because you didn't tell us not to, we are going to do it again. Like right now.

But this year we have a bit more detail for you. And by "you," I mean those of you who are loyal enough in your support to actually read a report like this. And by "a bit more detail" I am talking about the kind of info that our behind-the-scenes worker bees can obtain, men who know how to squeeze data out of various cyber-sources, the same way you might be able to wring out a wet washcloth. That accounts for why this year's report contains quite a bit more precise information, and why there is more water on the counter.

Let's start with the giveaways. This year we gave away 19,000 new books. This was a lower number than last year, but there is a good reason for that. Seven out of the thirteen books that we offered this year were repeat offers from last year, and those titles had already been given away a bunch in the previous go round (to the tune of 26,454).

The quantity of our traffic was a bit down this year, while the quality of engagement was way up. For the blog posts themselves, the bounce rate last year was 57% while this year it was 29%. People this year came purposefully, and they came to read. More than that, they came to read *words*.

In the video advertising we did for NQN, the number of new folks who watched it all the way through almost doubled from last year, and this was done on the same advertising budget.

Audio consumption was way up. There were 157,254 audio downloads of Blog and Mablog over 13 posts, meaning roughly 12,096 people took in these unqualified musings via the ear canal.

Last year *The NQN 2018 Anthology* sold almost a thousand copies within a week of release. Given how many of you are audiophiles concerning your audio files, we are planning to release this anthology as an audio book also.

The promo video for NQN 2019 was widely viewed, and I am rounding up or down here to the nearest K. There were 12K views on YouTube, 127K on Facebook, 2K on Instagram, and 20K on Twitter, for a grand total of 161K. There are even rumors of a possible Oscar. I won't say who is circulating these rumors, or even if me muttering under my breath constitutes a rumor, but rumors *are* circulating. Nancy keeps calling out to me from the other room, "Doug, did you say something?"

A rising tide floats all the boats, as they say, and the increased activity registered with some of our other projects as well. As many of you know, I have a weekly podcast called *The Plodcast*, and there were 79K downloads in November. One of them, the one about the banning of plastic straws in California, set a record for the Plodcast, with downloads in the neighborhood of 17K.

We also released season one of *Man Rampant* on Amazon Prime during this time, and the metric for this one is a little different, so bear with me. With streaming platforms like this, the most relevant stat in use here is how many minutes have been watched. Thus far we are past a million minutes viewed, and are averaging about 15,000 minutes a day.

And So What?

Now for anybody who is aware of the stats for all the Internet big boys, all of the above is what might be called chump change. So why am I touting these numbers as though they were in any way significant? And the answer is that these numbers are large enough to be significant within a particular theological ecosystem, and that is the Reformed evangelical ecosystem is that is trying very hard to pretend, and without registering too much discomposure, that I do not exist. For example, during this last month, there was a Reformed Pub dust-up, wherein people were exiled simply for mentioning my name.

Part of the reason for NQN is to break the existing embargo, and this reason relates nicely to the major strategic reason for all this that will be outlined at the end of this post. NQN last year was a nice beginning for all that, and this year we saw the once tight embargo becoming quite porous.

If you went back and read last year's *post mortem*, you should remember how I mentioned the troll guardians. Last year, if somebody retweeted something I said or did, the guardians would be all over it, claiming that I deny *sola fide*, or something else outrageous. And so let's just say they were quite a bit busier this year, firing away with the accuracy of epileptic storm troopers. We get quite the laser show, and with no injuries.

What Interested You Guys

What were the most popular posts this year? Coming in at number one was *Restoring Sexism: the Lost Virtue* (12,942 views). The silver medal goes to *The Grace of White Privilege* (12,2002), and the bronze to *A Word in Defense of Rosaria, If I May* (11,809). On this last item, I recently saw that *Pulpit & Pen* published an exposé of Rosaria, which cannot really be described as jumping the shark. No, it is more like jumping the sharknado.

In the category of "longest read posts"—recognizing of course that this could be a function of gripping prose *or* it could also be a function of overinflated wordiness that took longer than it should have to finish—we have three different posts to honor. First place was captured by *REZ ZOH LOOO TION #9* (with an average of 19.22 minutes). *Exceptions and Loopholes* (average of 16.48 minutes) took second, and *Rabshakeh, Chief of the Pronoun Police* (average of 13.11 minutes).

In a different drummer sort of thing, *Rabshekeh* also won the honors in another category, that category being the "most copied text."

Our Friend, Chris Wiley, and the Point of it All

Chris Wiley was out here in late October on a secret mission for her majesty the queen, and while he was here, we roped him into doing a few extra things. In fact, he was even present at the filming of the NQN video. He is, in other words, in a position to *know*.

Early on in November I saw a comment about NQN that he made on Facebook, a comment that I thought was very astute. "What was an astute comment doing on Facebook?" you might ask, and I understand your confusion. I am sure the authorities are looking into it. But at any rate, he said something astute about how it seemed to him that NQN was all about moving the Overton window. And yes, yes it is.

The Overton window defines the range of acceptable public discourse. If your position or proposal falls inside the window, then people will say, even when they differ, that it is "common sense," or "bipartisan," or "mainstream," or "challenging." If it is outside the window, then it will be dismissed as "extreme," or "unthinkable," or "radical," or "unacceptable." What has happened in the last decade or so is that the Overton window has slid drastically and most remarkably to the left. Part of the reason for this drastic shift is that the left decided to shoot the moon, and so they began to summarily declare any position outside of their own as being, by definition, outside the window. The totalitarianism embedded at the heart of their system has now emerged, and regular people can see how ugly it is.

I say the Overton window has moved. What do I mean? For example, and there are *many* examples, let us hypothetically take a 250-pound weight-lifter and mixed martial arts fighter named George Pounder III who suddenly announces that he is now a woman, Georgiana, and he starts entering women's weight-lifting competitions in order to win them all, and he enters the ring in order to begin destroying his opponents.

Now the fact that this could even happen is an indication that the window has moved, but the conclusive proof that the window has really moved is this. If a sportscaster were to say on air, or even privately in a hot mic moment, that he did not think this was "fair," he would probably lose his job. And if he didn't lose his job, it would only be the result of *him* abandoning his masculinity and crawling on his belly for a suitable time, like a Labrador retriever that had just been caught chewing on a slipper. Mark it. What virtually everybody *thought* just a few years ago is now what? That is right, *unthinkable*.

And sad to say, the evangelical establishment, the establishment running the embargo on us, acquiesces in this kind of thing. Anybody who uses phrases like *sexual minorities* is acquiescing. Anybody who gives a pass to conferences like Revoice, where labels like LGBTQ+ are thrown around, is acquiescing. What does that + stand for again? "We don't care, just so long as it is a sexual minority! We don't care, just so long as regular people think its sick!"

The reason I am so radical is not because I have somehow *become* a radical. I have become radical because I have simply remained where I was. You know, born in 1953, and all the girls in my class were girls, and all the boys in my class were boys, and I somehow got stuck in my ways. When the Overton window is moving the way it is, you can either move with it, and with the times, or you can sit there and find yourselves thinking unthinkable thoughts soon enough, even though you have thought that way your entire life.

Because evangelicals have made a fetish out of being winsome (perhaps that is what the + sign means?), they have not wanted to challenge *anything*. If they challenge this movement, they might be dismissed. If they confront the cultural apostasy, perhaps they will lose influence.

Look. You have lost more than enough influence already. Don't tell us how to not lose influence.

So NQN is a way of saying to all and sundry that we will continue to think our unthinkable thoughts. We will continue to say our unspeakable things. We will continue to treasure in our consciences our unconscionable things. And you can't stop us.

Made in the USA
Columbia, SC
15 October 2022